CAERIMONIA GRIMORIUM

SEPHER YETZIRAH

———————

GRIMORIUM VERUM

———————

GRIMOIRE OF TURIEL

———————

THE BLACK PULLET

———————

GRIMOIRE OF HONORIOUS

CONTENTS

SEPHER YETZIRAH

INTRODUCTION

THE BOOK OF FORMATION

CHAPTER I

CHAPTER II

CHAPTER III
The Three Mothers

CHAPTER IV
The Seven Double Letters

CHAPTER V
The Twelve Simple Letters

CHAPTER VI

THE FIFTY GATES OF INTELLIGENCE
First Order: Elementary
Second Order: Decad of Evolution
Third Order: Decad of Humanity
Fourth Order: World of Spheres
Fifth Order: The Angelic World
Sixth Order: The Archtype
The Thirty-Two Paths of Wisdom

NOTES TO THE SEPHER YETZIRAH
Chapter I
Chapter II
Chapter III
Chapter IV
Chapter V

Chapter VI

NOTES TO THE THIRTY-TWO PATHS OF WISDOM

GRIMOIRIUM VERUM

INTRODUCTION

THE FIRST BOOK
Concerning the Characters of the Daemons
Of the Nature of Pacts
The Kinds of Spirits
The Visible Appearance of Spirits
To Invoke the Spirits
Descending to the Spirits

THE SECOND BOOK
Agla Adonay Jehova

THE THIRD BOOK
The Invocation
Orison: Preparation
Of the Magical Knife
Conjuration of the Instrument
The Sacrificial Knife
The Manner of Asperging & Fumigation
Of the Virgin Parchment
Orison
Of the Lancet
Invocation
The Benediction of the Salt
The Orison of the Stones
Of the Aspersion of the Water
Of Aspersion
Of the Perfumes
The Orison of the Aromatic Perfumes

Of the Pen of the Art
The Ink-Horn
The Preparation of the Operator
Invocation to Scrilin
Conjuration for Lucifer
Conjuration for Beelzebuth
Conjuration for Astaroth
Conjuration for Inferior Spirits
Dismissal of the Inferior Spirits
Orison of the Salamanders
Of the Pentacle and the Manner of Working
Dismissal of the Spirit
A Rare & Surprising Magical Secret
Dismissing the Spirit
Divination by the Word of Uriel
The Conjuration
Divination by the Egg
To See Spirits of the Air
To Make Girls or Gentlemen Appear in your Room, After Supper
To Make a Girl Come to You, However Modest She May Be
The Conjuration
To Make Oneself Invisible
To Have Gold or Silver or the Hand of Glory
Garters for Distances
To Make a Girl Dance in the Nude
To See in a Vision Anything From the Past or Future
Orison
To Nail (an Enemy)

THE SECRET GRIMOIRE OF TURIEL

PART THE FIRST

First Morning Prayer
The Blessing of the Light
Consecration of the Sword
Benediction of the Lamens
Benediction of the Pentacles
Benediction of the Garment
Benediction of the Perfumes
Exorcism of Fire
Invocation for Sunday
Invocation for Monday
Invocation for Tuesday
Invocation for Wednesday
Invocation for Thursday
Invocation for Friday
Invocation for Saturday
Character of Aratron Lord of Saturn
Character of Praleg Lord of Mars
Character of Phul Lord of the Moon
Character of Jethor Lord of Jupiter
Character of Ophiel Lord of Mercury
Character of Hagith Lord of Venus
Character of Och Lord of the Sun

PART THE SECOND
Containing Invocations, Conjuration, Aro Exorcisms of tree Band of Spirits
Form of Conjuring and Exorcising Spirits
Prayer
Names and Offices of the Spirits Messengers and Intelligences of the Seven Planets
Invocation
Interrogations

THE BLACK PULLET

PREFACE

THE BLACK PULLET
Oration of the Sages
First Prayer
Second Prayer

THE GRIMIORE OF HONORIUS

Prayer
Prayer
The Seventy-two Sacred Names of God
The Beginning of the Holy Gospel according to John
Universal Conjuration
The Grand Pentacle of Salomon
Act of Thanksgiving
Conjuration of the Book
Conjuration of the Demons
Concerning the Figure of the Circle
The Magic Circle of Honorius
Conjuration of the King of the East
Conjuration of the King of the South
Conjuration of the King of the West
Conjuration of the King of the North

CONJURATION FOR EACH DAY OF THE WEEK

SEPHER YETZIRAH

SEPHER YETZIRAH

TRANSLATED FROM THE ORIGINAL HEBREW BY WILLIAM WYNN WESTCOTT

The Sepher Yetzirah *is one of the most famous of the ancient Qabalistic texts. It was first put into writing around 200 AD. Westcott's Translation of the* Sepher Yetzirah *was a primary source for the rituals and Knowledge Lectures of the Golden Dawn. This is the Third Edition of Westcott's translation, first published in 1887.*

INTRODUCTION

The "Sepher Yetzirah," or "Book of Formation," is perhaps the oldest Rabbinical treatise of Kabalistic philosophy which is still extant. The great interest which has been evinced of late years in the Hebrew Kabalah, and the modes of thought and doctrine allied to it, has induced me to translate this tractate from the original Hebrew texts, and to collate with them the Latin versions of mediaeval authorities; and I have also published *An Introduction to the Kabalah* which may be found useful to students.

Three important books of the "Zohar," or "Book of Splendor," which is a great storehouse of Kabalistic teaching, have been translated into English by S. L. MacGregor Mathers, and the "Sepher Yetzirah" in an English translation is almost a necessary companion to these abstruse disquisitions: the two books indeed mutually explain each other.

The "Sepher Yetzirah," although this name means "The Book of Formation," is not in any sense a narrative of Creation, or a substitute Genesis, but is an ancient and instructive philosophical treatise upon one aspect of the origin of the universe and mankind; an aspect at once archaic and essentially Hebrew. The grouping of the processes of origin into an arrangement, at once alphabetic and numeral, is one only to be found in Semitic authors. Attention must be called to the essential peculiarity of the Hebrew language, the inextricable and necessary association of numbers and letters; every letter suggesting a number, and every group of letters having a numerical signification, as vital as its literal meaning. The Kabalistic principles involved in the reversal of Hebrew letters, and their substitution by others, on definite schemes, should also be studied and borne in mind.

It is exactly on these principles that the "ground-work idea" 'of this disquisition rests; and these principles may be traced throughout the Kabalistic tractates which have succeeded it in point of time and development, many of which are associated together in one volume known as the "Zohar," which is in the main concerned with the essential dignities of the Godhead, with the Emanations which have sprung therefrom, with the doctrine of the Sephiroth, the ideals of Macroprosopus and Microprosopus, and the doctrine of Re-incarnation.

The "Sepher Yetzirah," on the other hand, is mainly concerned with our universe and with the Microcosm. The opinions of Hebrew Kabalistic Rabbis and of modern mystics may be fitly introduced here. The following interesting quotation is from Rabbi Moses Botarel, who wrote his famous Commentary in 1409:--"It was Abraham our Father--blessed be he--who wrote this book to condemn the doctrine of the sages of his time, who were incredulous of the supreme dogma of the Unity. At least, this was the opinion of Rabbi Saadiah--blessed be he--as written in the first chapter of his book *The Philosopher's Stone*. These are his words: The sages of Babylon attacked Abraham on account of his faith; for they were all against him although themselves separable into three sects. The First thought that the Universe was subject to the control of two opposing forces, the one existing but to destroy the other, this is dualism; they held that there was nothing in common between the author of evil and the author of good. The Second sect admitted Three great Powers; two of them as in the first case, and a third Power whose function was to decide between the two others, a supreme arbitrator. The Third sect recognized no god beside the Sun, in which it recognized the sole principle of existence."

Rabbi Judah Ha Lévi (who flourished about 1120), in his critical description of this treatise, wrote: "The Sepher Yetzirah teaches us the existence of a Single Divine Power by showing us that in the bosom of variety and multiplicity there is a Unity and Harmony, and that such universal concord could only arise from the rule of a Supreme Unity." According to Isaac Myer, in his *Quabbalah* (p. 159), the "Sepher Yetzirah" was referred to in the writings of Ibn Gebirol of Cordova, commonly called Avicebron, who died in A.D. 1070.

Eliphas Levi, the famous French Occultist, thus wrote of the "Sepher Yetzirah," in his *Histoire de la Magie*, p. 54: "The Zohar is a Genesis of illumination, the Sepher Jezirah is a ladder formed of truths. Therein are explained the thirty-two absolute signs of sounds, numbers and letters: each letter reproduces a number, an idea and a form; so that mathematics are capable of application to ideas and to forms not less rigorously than to numbers, by exact proportion and perfect correspondence. By the science of the Sepher Jezirah the human spirit is fixed to truth, and in reason, and is able to take account of the possible development of intelligence by the evolutions of numbers. The Zohar represents absolute truth, and the Sepher Jezirah provides the means by which we may seize, appropriate and make use of it."

Upon another page Eliphas Lévi writes: "The Sepher Jezirah and the Apocalypse are the masterpieces of Occultism; they contain more wisdom than words; their expression is as figurative as poetry, and at the same time it is as exact as mathematics. In the volume entitled *La Kabbale* by the eminent French scholar, Adolphe Franck, there is a chapter on the "Sepher Yetzirah." He writes as follows:

"The Book of Formation contains, I will not say system of physics, but of cosmology such as could be conceived at an age and in a country where the habit of explaining all phenomena by the immediate action of the First Cause, tended to check the spirit of observation, and where in consequence certain general and superficial relations perceived in the natural world passed for the science of Nature."..."Its form is simple and grave; there is nothing like a demonstration nor an argument; but it consists rather of a series of aphorisms, regularly grouped, and which have all the conciseness of the most ancient oracles."

In his analysis of the "Sepher Yetzirah," he adds:--"The Book of Formation, even if it be not very voluminous, and if it do not altogether raise us to very elevated regions of thought, yet offers us at least a composition which is very homogeneous and of a rare originality. The clouds which the imagination of commentators have gathered around it, will be dissipated, if we look for, in it, not mysteries of ineffable wisdom, but an attempt at a reasonable doctrine, made when reason arose, an effort to grasp the plan of the universe, and to secure the link which binds to one common principle, all the elements which are around us. The last word of this system is the substitution of the absolute divine Unity for every idea of Dualism, for that pagan philosophy which saw in matter an eternal substance whose laws were not in accord with Divine Will; and for the Biblical doctrine, which by its idea of Creation, postulates two things, the Universe and God, as two substances absolutely distinct one from the other. In fact, in the 'Sepher Yetzirah,' God considered as the Infinite and consequently the indefinable Being, extended throughout all things by his power and existence, is while above, yet not outside of numbers, sounds and letters--the principles and general laws which we recognize. "Every element has its source from a higher form, and all things have their common origin from the Word (*Logos*), the Holy Spirit.... So God is at once, in the highest sense, both the matter and the form of the universe. Yet He is not *only* that form; for nothing can or does exist outside of Himself; His substance is the foundation of all, and all things bear His imprint and are symbols of His intelligence."

Hebrew tradition assigns the doctrines of the oldest portions of the "Zohar" to a date antecedent to the building of the Second Temple, but Rabbi Simeon ben Jochai, who lived in the reign of the Emperor Titus, A.D. 70-80, is considered to have been the first to commit these to writing, and Rabbi Moses de Leon, of Guadalaxara, in Spain, who died in 1305, certainly reproduced and published the "Zohar."

Ginsburg, speaking of the Zoharic doctrines of the Ain Suph, says that they were unknown until the thirteenth century, but he does not deny the great antiquity of the "Sepher Yetzirah," in which it will be noticed the "Ain Suph Aur" and "Ain Suph" are not mentioned. I suggest, however, that this omission is no proof that the doctrines of "Ain Suph Aur" and "Ain Suph" did not then exist, because it is a reasonable supposition that the "Sepher Yetzirah" was the volume assigned to the Yetziratic World, the third of the four Kabalistic Worlds of Emanation, while the "Asch Metzareph" is concerned with the Assiatic, fourth, or lowest World of Shells, and is on the face of it an alchemical treatise; and again the "Siphra Dtzenioutha" may be fittingly considered to be an Aziluthic work, treating of the Emanations of Deity alone; and there was doubtless a fourth work assigned to the World of Briah--the second type, but I have not been able to identify this treatise. Both the Babylonian and the Jerusalem Talmuds refer to the "Sepher Yetzirah." Their treatise, named "Sanhedrin," certainly mentions the "Book of Formation," and another similar work; and Rashi in his commentary on the treatise "Erubin," considers this a reliable historical notice. Other historical notices are those of Saadya Gaon, who died A.D. 940, and Judah Ha Levi, A.D. 1150; both these Hebrew classics speak of it as a very ancient work. Some modern critics have attributed the authorship to the Rabbi Akiba, who lived in the time of the Emperor Hadrian, A.D. 120, and lost his life in supporting the claims of Barchocheba, a false messiah: others suggest it was first written about A.D. 200.

Graetz however assigns it to early Gnostic times, third or fourth century, and Zunz speaks of it as post Talmudical, and belonging to the Geonim period 700-800 A.D.; Rubinsohn, in the *Bibliotheca Sacra*, speaks of this latter idea as having no real basis. The Talmuds were first collected into a concrete whole, and printed in Venice, 1520 A.D.

The "Zohar" was first printed in Mantua in 1558; again in Cremona, 1560; and at Lublin, 1623; and a fourth edition by Knorr von Rosenroth, at Sulzbach in 1684. Some parts are not very ancient, because the Crusades are mentioned in one chapter. Six extant Hebrew editions of the "Sepher Yetzirah" were collected and printed at Lemberg in 1680. The oldest of these six recensions was that of Saadjah Gaon (by some critics called spurious). There are still extant three Latin versions, *viz.*, that of Gulielmus Postellus; one by Johann Pistorius; and a third by Joannes Stephanus

Rittangelius; this latter gives both Hebrew and Latin versions, and also "The Thirty-Two Paths" as a supplement.

There is a German translation, by Johann Friedrich von Meyer, dated 1830; a version by Isidor Kalisch, in which he has reproduced many of the valuable annotations of Meyer; an edition in French by Papus, 1888; an edition in French by Mayer Lambert, 1891, with the Arabic Commentary of Saadya Gaon; and an English edition by Peter Davidson, 1896, to which are added "The Fifty Gates of Intelligence" and "The Thirty-Two Ways of Wisdom." The edition which I now offer is fundamentally that of the ancient Hebrew codices translated into English, and collated with the Latin versions of Pistorius, Postellus, and Rittangelius, following the latter, rather than the former commentators. As to the authenticity of "The Sepher Yetzirah," students may refer to the *Bibliotheca magna Rabbinica* of Bartoloccio de Cellerio, Rome, 1678-1692; to Basnage, *History of the Jews*, 1708; and to *The Doctrine and Literature of the Kabalah*, by A. B. Waite, 1902.

The "Sepher Yetzirah" consists of six chapters, having 33 paragraphs distributed among them, in this manner: the first has 12, then follow 5, 5, 4, 3, and 4. Yet in some versions the paragraphs and subject-matter are found in a different arrangement. The oldest title has, as an addition, the words, "The Letters of our Father Abraham" or "ascribed to the patriarch Abraham," and it is spoken of as such by many mediaeval authorities: but this origin is doubtless fabulous, although perhaps not more improbable than the supposed authorship of the "Book of Enoch," mentioned by St. Jude, of which two MSS. copies in the Ethiopic language were rescued from the wilds of Abyssinia in 1773 by the great traveller James Bruce. In essence this work was, doubtless, the crystallisation of centuries of tradition, by one writer, and it has been added to from time to time, by later authors, who have also revised it. Some of the additions, which were rejected even by mediaeval students, I have not incorporated with the text at all, and I present in this volume only the undoubted kernel of this occult nut, upon which many great authorities, Hebrew, German, Jesuit and others, have written long Commentaries, and yet have failed to explain satisfactorily. I find Kalisch, speaking of these Commentaries, says, "they contain nothing but a medley of arbitrary explanations, and sophistical distortions of scriptural verses, astrological notions, Oriental superstitions, a metaphysical jargon, a poor knowledge of physics, and not a correct elucidation of this ancient book." Kalisch, however, was not an occultist; these commentaries are, however, so extensive as to demand years of study, and I feel no hesitation in confessing that my researches into them have been but superficial. For convenience of study I have placed the Notes in a separate form at the end of the work, and I have made a short definition of the subject-matter of each chapter. The substance of this little volume was read as Lecture before "The Hermetic Society of London," in the summer of 1886, Dr. Anna Kingsford, President, in the chair. Some of the Notes were the explanations given verbally, and subsequently in writing, to members of the Society who asked for information upon abstruse points in the "Sepher," and for collateral doctrines; others, of later date, are answers which have been given to students of Theosophy and Hermetic philosophy, and to my pupils of the Study Groups of the Rosicrucian Society of England.

SEPHER YETZIRAH

(The Book of Formation)

CHAPTER I

1. In thirty-two ⁽¹⁾ mysterious Paths of Wisdom did Jah, ⁽²⁾ the Jehovah of hosts, ⁽³⁾ the God of Israel, ⁽⁴⁾ the Living Elohim, ⁽⁵⁾ the King of ages, the merciful and gracious God, ⁽⁶⁾ the Exalted One, the Dweller in eternity, most high and holy--engrave his name by the three Sepharim ⁽⁷⁾ --Numbers, Letters, and Sounds.⁽⁸⁾

2. Ten are the ineffable Sephiroth. ⁽⁹⁾ Twenty-two are the Letters, the Foundation of all things; there are Three Mothers, Seven Double and Twelve ⁽¹⁰⁾ Simple letters.

3. The ineffable Sephiroth are Ten, as are the Numbers; and as there are in man five fingers over against five, so over them is established a covenant of strength, by word of mouth, and by the circumcision of the flesh. ⁽¹¹⁾

4. Ten is the number of the ineffable Sephiroth, ten and not nine, ten and not eleven. Understand this wisdom, and be wise by the perception. Search out concerning it, restore the Word to its creator, and replace Him who formed it upon his throne. ⁽¹²⁾

5. The Ten ineffable Sephiroth have ten vast regions bound unto them; boundless in origin and having no ending; an abyss ⁽¹³⁾ of good and of ill; measureless height and depth; boundless to the East and the West; boundless to the North and South; ⁽¹⁴⁾ and the Lord the only God, ⁽¹⁵⁾ the Faithful King rules all these from his holy seat, ⁽¹⁶⁾ for ever and ever.

6. The Ten ineffable Sephiroth have the appearance of the Lightning flash, [17] their origin is unseen and no end is perceived. The Word is in them as they rush forth and as they return, they speak as from the whirl-wind, and returning fall prostrate in adoration before the Throne.

7. The Ten ineffable Sephiroth, whose ending is even as their origin, are like as a flame arising from a burning coal. For God [18] is superlative in his Unity, there is none equal unto Him: what number canst thou place before One.

8. Ten are the ineffable Sephiroth; seal up thy lips lest thou speak of them, and guard thy heart as thou considerest them; and if thy mind escape from thee bring it back to thy control; even as it was said, "running and returning" (the living creatures ran and returned) [19] and hence was the Covenant made.

9. The ineffable Sephiroth give forth the Ten numbers. First; the Spirit of the God of the living; [20] Blessed and more than blessed be the Living God [21] of ages. The Voice, the Spirit, and the Word, [22] these are the Holy Spirit.

10. Second; from the Spirit He produced Air, and formed in it twenty-two sounds--the letters; three are mothers, seven are double, and twelve are simple; but the Spirit is first and above these. Third; from the Air He formed the Waters, and from the formless and void [23] made mire and clay, and designed surfaces upon them, and hewed recesses in them, and formed the strong material foundation. Fourth; from the Water He formed Fire [24] and made for Himself a Throne of Glory with Auphanim, Seraphim and Kerubim, [25] as his ministering angels; and with these three [26] he completed his dwelling, as it is written, "Who maketh his angels spirits and his ministers a flaming fire." [27]

11. He selected three letters from among the simple ones and sealed them and formed them into a Great Name, I H V, [28] and with this He sealed the universe in six directions.

Fifth; He looked above, and sealed the Height with I H V.

Sixth; He looked below, and sealed the Depth with I V H.

Seventh; He looked forward, and sealed the East with H I V.

Eighth; He looked backward, and sealed the West with H V I.

Ninth; He looked to the right, and sealed the South with V I H.

Tenth; He looked to the left, and sealed the North with V H I.

12. Behold! From the Ten ineffable Sephiroth do, proceed--the One Spirit of the Gods of the living, Air, Water, Fire; and also Height, Depth, East, West, South and North. [29]

CHAPTER II

1. The twenty-two sounds and letters are the Foundation of all things. Three mothers, seven doubles and twelve simples. The Three Mothers are Aleph, Mem and Shin, they are Air, Water and Fire Water is silent, Fire is sibilant, and Air derived from the Spirit is as the tongue of a balance standing between these contraries which are in equilibrium, reconciling and mediating between them.

2. He hath formed, weighed, and composed with these twenty-two letters every created thing, and the form of everything which shall hereafter be.

3. These twenty-two sounds or letters are formed by the voice, impressed on the air, and audibly modified in five places; in the throat, in the mouth, by the tongue, through the teeth, and by the lips. [31]

4. These twenty-two letters, which are the foundation of all things, He arranged as upon a sphere with two hundred and thirty-one gates, and the sphere may be rotated forward or backward, whether for good or for evil; from the good comes true pleasure, from evil nought but torment.

5. For He shewed the combination of these letters, each with the other; Aleph with all, and all with Aleph; Beth with all, and all with Beth. Thus in combining all together in pairs are produced the two hundred and thirty-one gates of knowledge. [32]

6. And from the non-existent [33] He made Something; and all forms of speech and everything that has been produced; from the empty void He made the material world, and from the inert earth He brought forth everything that hath life. He hewed, as it were, vast columns out of the intangible air, and by the power of His Name made every creature and everything that is; and the production of all things from the twenty-two letters is the proof that they are all but parts of one living body. [34]

CHAPTER III

THE THREE MOTHERS

1. The Foundation of all the other sounds and letters is provided by the Three Mothers, Aleph, Mem and Shin (A,M,C); they resemble a Balance, on the one hand the guilty, on the other hand the purified, and Aleph the Air is like the Tongue of a Balance standing between them. (35)

2. The Three Mothers, Aleph, Mem and Shin, are a great Mystery, very admirable and most recondite, and sealed as with six rings; and from them proceed Air, Fire, and Water, which divide into active and passive forces. The Three Mothers, Aleph, Mem and Shin, are the Foundation, from them spring three Fathers, and from these have proceeded all things that are in the world.

3. The Three Mothers in the world are Aleph, Mem and Shin: the heavens (36) were produced (37) from Fire; the earth from the Water; and the Air from the Spirit is as a reconciler between the Fire and the Water.

4. The Three Mothers, Aleph, Mem and Shin, Fire, Water and Air, are shown in the Year: from the fire came heat, from the waters came cold, and from the air was produced the temperate state, again a mediator between them. The Three Mothers, Aleph, Mem and Shin, Fire, Water and Air, are found in Man: from the fire was

formed the head; from the water the belly; and from the air was formed the chest, again placed as a mediator between the others.

5. These Three Mothers did He produce and design, and combined them; and He sealed them as the three mothers in the Universe, in the Year and in Man--both male and female. He caused the letter Aleph to reign in Air and crowned it, and combining it with the others He sealed it, as Air in the World, as the temperate (climate) of the Year, and as the breath in the chest (the lungs for breathing air) in Man: the male with Aleph, Mem, Shin, the female with Shin, Mem, Aleph. He caused the letter Mem to reign in Water, crowned it, and combining it with the others formed the earth in the world, cold in the year, and the belly in man, male and female, the former with Mem, Aleph, Shin, the latter with Mem, Shin, Aleph. He caused Shin to reign in Fire, and crowned it, and combining it with the others sealed with it the heavens in the universe, heat in the year and the head in man, male and female. [38]

CHAPTER IV

THE SEVEN DOUBLE LETTERS

1. The Seven double letters, Beth, Gimel, Daleth, Kaph, Peh, Resh, and Tau (b,g,d,k,p,r,t) have each two sounds associated with them. They are referred to Life, Peace, Wisdom, Riches, Grace, Fertility and Power. The two sounds of each letter are the hard and the soft--the aspirated and the softened. They are called Double, because each letter presents a contrast or permutation; thus Life and Death; Peace and War; Wisdom and Folly; Riches and Poverty; Grace and Indignation; Fertility and Solitude; Power and Servitude.

2. These Seven Double Letters point out seven localities; Above, Below, East, West, North, South, and the Palace of Holiness in the midst of them sustaining all things.

3. These Seven Double Letters He designed, produced, and combined, and formed with them the Planets of this World, the Days of the Week, and the Gates of the soul (the orifices of perception) in Man. From these Seven He bath produced the Seven Heavens, the Seven Earths, the Seven Sabbaths: for this cause He has loved and blessed the number Seven more than all things under Heaven (His Throne).

4. Two Letters produce two houses; three form six; four form twenty-four; five form one hundred and twenty; six form seven

hundred and twenty; [39] seven form five thousand and forty; and beyond this their numbers increase so that the mouth can hardly utter them, nor the ear hear the number of them. So now, behold the Stars of our World, the Planets which are Seven; the Sun, Venus, Mercury, Moon, Saturn, Jupiter and Mars. The Seven are also the Seven Days of Creation; and the Seven Gateways of the Soul of Man--the two eyes, the two ears, the mouth and the two nostrils. So with the Seven are formed the seven heavens, [41] the seven earths, and the seven periods of time; and so has He preferred the number Seven above all things under His Heaven. [42]

SUPPLEMENT TO CHAPTER IV

NOTE.--This is one of several modern illustrations of the allotment of the Seven Letters; it is not found in the ancient copies of the "Sepher Yetzirah."

He produced Beth, and referred it to Wisdom ; He crowned it, combined and formed with it the Moon in the Universe, the first day of the week, and the right eye of man.

He produced Gimel, and referred it to Health; He crowned it, combined and joined with it Mars in the Universe, the second day of the week, and the right ear of man.

He produced Daleth, and referred it to Fertility; He crowned it, combined and formed with it the Sun in the Universe, the third day of the week, and the right nostril of man.

He produced Kaph, and referred it to Life; He crowned it, combined and formed with it Venus in the Universe, the fourth day of the week, and the left eye of man.

He produced Peh, and referred it to Power; He crowned it, combined and formed with it Mercury in the Universe, the fifth day of the week, and the left ear of man.

He produced Resh, and referred it to Peace; He crowned it, combined and formed with it Saturn in the Universe, the sixth day of the week, and the left nostril of man.

He produced Tau, and referred it to Beauty; He crowned it, combined and formed with it Jupiter in the Universe, the Seventh Day of the week, and the mouth of man.

By these Seven letters were also made seven worlds, seven heavens, seven earths, seven seas, seven rivers, seven deserts, seven days, seven weeks from Passover to Pentecost, and every seventh year a Jubilee.

Mayer Lambert gives:--Beth to Saturn and the Hebrew Sabbath-- that is Saturday; Gimel to Jupiter and Sunday; Daleth to Mars and Monday; Kaph to the Sun and Tuesday; Peh to Venus and Wednesday; Resh to Mercury and Thursday; and Tau to the Moon and Friday.

CHAPTER V

THE TWELVE SIMPLE LETTERS

1. The Twelve Simple Letters are Héh, Vau, Zain, Cheth, Teth, Yod, Lamed, Nun, Samech, Oin, Tzaddi and Qoph (h,w,z,j,f,y,l,n,s,u,x,q); [43] they are the foundations of these twelve properties: Sight, Hearing, Smell, Speech, Taste, Sexual Love, Work, Movement, Anger, Mirth, Imagination, [44] and Sleep. These Twelve are also allotted to the directions in space: North-east, South-east, the East above, the East below, the North above, the North below, the South-west, the Northwest, the West above, the West below, the South above, and the South below; these diverge to infinity, and are as the arms of the Universe.

2. These Twelve Simple Letters He designed, and combined, and formed with them the Twelve celestial constellations of the Zodiac, whose signs are Teth, Shin, Tau, Samech, Aleph, Beth, Mem, Oin, Qoph, Gimel, Daleth, and Daleth. [45] The Twelve are also the Months of the Year: Nisan, [46] Yiar, Sivan, Tamuz, Ab, Elul, Tishri, Hesvan, Kislev, Tebet, Sabat and Adar. The Twelve are also the Twelve organs of living creatures: [47] the two hands, the two feet, the two kidneys, the spleen, the liver, the gall, private parts, stomach and intestines.

He made these, as it were provinces, and arranged them as in order of battle for warfare. And also the Elohim [48] made one from the region of the other.

Three Mothers and Three Fathers; and thence issue Fire, Air and Water. Three Mothers, Seven Doubles and Twelve Simple letters and sounds.

3. Behold now these are the Twenty and Two Letters from which Jah, Jehovah Tzabaoth, the Living Elohim, the God of Israel, exalted and sublime, the Dweller in eternity, formed and established all things; High and Holy is His Name.

SUPPLEMENT TO CHAPTER V

NOTE.--This is a modern illustration of the allotment of the Twelve Letters; it is not found in the ancient copies of the "Sepher Yetzirah."

1. God produced Hé predominant in Speech, crowned it, combined and formed with it Aries in the Universe, Nisan in the Year, and the right foot of Man.

2. He produced Vau, predominant in mind, crowned it, combined and formed with it Taurus in the Universe, Aiar in the Year, and the right kidney of Man.

3. He produced Zain, predominant in Movement crowned it, combined and formed it with Gemini in the Universe, Sivan in the Year, and the left foot of Man.

4. He produced Cheth, predominant in Sight, crowned it, combined and formed it with Cancer in the Universe, Tammuz in the year, and the right hand of Man.

5. He produced Teth, predominant in Hearing, crowned it, combined and formed with it Leo in the Universe, Ab in the Year, and the left kidney in Man.

6. He produced Yod, predominant in Work, crowned it, combined and formed with it Virgo in the Universe, Elul in the Year, and the left hand of Man.

7. He produced Lamed, predominant in Sexual desire, crowned it, combined and formed with it Libra in the Universe, Tishri in the Year, and the private parts of Man. (Kalisch gives "gall.")

8. He produced Nun, predominant in Smell, crowned it, combined and formed with it Scorpio in the Universe, Heshvan in the Year, and the intestines of Man.

9. He produced Samech, predominant in Sleep, crowned it, combined and formed with it Sagittarius in the Universe, Kislev in the Year, and the stomach of Man.

10. He produced Oin, predominant in Anger, crowned it, combined and formed with it Capricornus in the Universe, Tebet in the Year, and the liver of Man.

11. He produced Tzaddi, predominant in Taste, crowned it, combined and formed with it Aquarius in the Year, and the gullet in Man).

12. He produced Qoph, predominant in Mirth, crowned it, combined and formed with it Pisces in the Universe, Adar in the Year, and the spleen of Man.

NOTE.--Mediaeval authorities and modern editors give very different allocations to the twelve simple letters.

CHAPTER VI

Section 1. Three Fathers and their generations, Seven conquerors and their armies, and Twelve bounds of the Universe. See now, of these words, the faithful witnesses are the Universe, the Year and Man. The dodecad, the heptad, and the triad with their provinces; above is the Celestial Dragon, T L I, [49] and below is the World, and lastly the heart of Man. The Three are Water, Air and Fire; Fire above, Water below, and Air conciliating between them; and the sign of these things is that the Fire sustains (volatilises) the waters; Mem is mute, Shin is sibilant, and Aleph is the Mediator and as it were a friend placed between them.

2. The Celestial Dragon, T L I, is placed over the universe like a king upon the throne; the revolution of the year is as a king over his dominion; the heart of man is as a king in warfare. Moreover, He made all things one from the other; and the Elohim set good over against evil, and made good things from good, and evil things from evil; with the good tested He the evil, and with the evil did He try the good. Happiness [50] is reserved for the good, and misery [51] is kept for the wicked.

3. The Three are One, and that One stands above. The Seven are divided; three are over against three, and one stands between the triads. The Twelve stand as in warfare; three are friends, three are enemies; three are life givers; three are destroyers. The three friends are the heart, the ears, and the mouth; the three enemies are the liver, the gall, and the tongue; [52] while God [53] the faithful

king rules over all. One above Three, Three above Seven, and Seven above Twelve: and all are connected the one with the other.

4. And after that our father Abraham had perceived and understood, and had taken down and engraved all these things, the Lord most high [55] revealed Himself, and called him His beloved, and made a Covenant with him and his seed; and Abraham believed on Him [56] and it was imputed unto him for righteousness. And He made this Covenant as between the ten toes of the feet--this is that of circumcision; and as between the ten fingers of the hands and this is that of the tongue. [57] And He formed the twenty-two letters into speech [58] and shewed him all the mysteries of them. [59] He drew them through the Waters; He burned them in the Fire; He vibrated them in the Air; Seven planets in the heavens, and Twelve celestial constellations of the stars of the Zodiac.

- End of "The Book of Formation"

THE FIFTY GATES OF INTELLIGENCE

Attached to some editions of the "Sepher Yetzirah" is found this scheme of Kabalistic classification of knowledge emanating from the Second Sephira Binah, Understanding, and descending by stages through the angels, heavens, humanity, animal and vegetable and mineral kingdoms to Hyle and the chaos. The Kabalists said that one must enter and pass up through the Gates to attain to the Thirty-two Paths of Wisdom; and that even Moses only passed through the forty-ninth Gate, and never entered the fiftieth.

FIRST ORDER:

ELEMENTARY

1. Chaos, Hyle, The first matter.

2. Formless, void, lifeless.

3. The Abyss.

4. Origin of the Elements.

5. Earth (no seed germs).

6. Water.

7. Air.

8. Fire

9. Differentiation of qualities.

10. Mixture and combination.

SECOND ORDER:

DECAD OF EVOLUTION

11. Minerals differentiate.

12. Vegetable principles appear.

13. Seeds germinate in moisture.

14. Herbs and Trees.

15. Fructification in vegetable life.

16. Origin of low forms of animal life.

17. Insects and Reptiles appear.

18. Fishes, vertebrate life in the waters.

19. Birds, vertebrate life in the air.

20. Quadrupeds, vertebrate earth animals.

THIRD ORDER:

DECAD OF HUMANITY

21. Appearance of Man.

22. Material human body.

23. Human Soul conferred.

24. Mystery of Adam and Eve.

25. Complete Man as the Microcosm.

26. Gift of five human faces acting exteriorly.

27. Gift of five powers to the soul.

28. Adam Kadmon, the Heavenly Man.

29. Angelic beings.

30. Man in the image of God.

FOURTH ORDER:

WORLD OF SPHERES

31. The Moon.

32. Mercury.

33. Venus.

34. Sol.

35. Mars.

36. Jupiter.

37. Saturn.

38. The Firmament.

39. The Primum Mobile.

40. The Empyrean Heaven.

FIFTH ORDER:

THE ANGELIC WORLD

41. Ishim--Sons of Fire.

42. Auphanim--Cherubim.

43. Aralim--Thrones.

44. Chashmalim--Dominions.

45. Seraphim--Virtues.

46. Malakim--Powers.

47. Elohim--Principalities.

48. Beni Elohim--Angels.

49. Cherubim--Arch-angels.

SIXTH ORDER:

THE ARCHETYPE

50. God. Ain Suph. He Whom no mortal eye bath seen, and Who has been known to Jesus the Messiah alone.

NOTE.--The Angels of the Fifth or Angelic World are arranged in very different order by various Kabalistic Rabbis.

THE THIRTY-TWO PATHS OF WISDOM

Translated from the Hebrew Text of Joannes Stephanus Rittangelius, 1642: which is also to be found in the "Oedipus Aegyptiacus" of Athanasius Kircher, 1653. These paragraphs are very obscure in meaning, and the Hebrew text is probably very corrupt.

The First Path is called the Admirable or the Hidden Intelligence (the Highest Crown): for it is the Light giving the power of comprehension of that First Principle which has no beginning; and it is the Primal Glory, for no created being can attain to its essence.

The Second Path is that of the Illuminating Intelligence: it is the Crown of Creation, the Splendour of the Unity, equalling it, and it is exalted above every head, and named by the Kabalists the Second Glory.

The Third Path is the Sanctifying Intelligence, and is the foundation of Primordial wisdom, which is called the Creator of Faith, and its roots are AMN; and it is the parent of Faith, from which doth Faith emanate.

The Fourth Path is named the Cohesive or Receptacular Intelligence; and is so called because it contains all the holy powers, and from it emanate all the spiritual virtues with the most exalted essences: they emanate one from the other by the power of the Primordial Emanation. The Highest Crown.) [1]

The Fifth Path is called the Radical Intelligence, because it resembles the Unity, uniting itself to the Binah, [2] or Intelligence which emanates from the Primordial depths of Wisdom or Chokmah. [3]

The Sixth Path is called the Mediating Intelligence, because in it are multiplied the influxes of the emanations, for it causes that influence to flow into all the reservoirs of the Blessings, with which these themselves are united.

The Seventh Path is the Occult Intelligence, because it is the Refulgent Splendour of all the Intellectual virtues which are perceived by the eyes of intellect, and by the contemplation of faith.

The Eighth Path is called the Absolute or Perfect Intelligence, because it is the means of the primordial, which has no root by which it can cleave, nor rest, except in the hidden places of *Gedulah*, [4] Magnificence, from which emanates its own proper essence.

The Ninth Path is the Pure Intelligence, so called because it purifies the Numerations, it proves and corrects the designing of their representation, and disposes their unity with which they are combined without diminution or division.

The Tenth Path is the Resplendent Intelligence, because it is exalted above every head, and sits on the throne of *Binah (the Intelligence spoken of in the Third Path)*. It illuminates the splendour of all the lights, and causes an influence to emanate from the Prince of countenances. [5]

The Eleventh Path is the Scintillating Intelligence, because it is the essence of that curtain which is placed close to the order of the disposition, and this is a special dignity given to it that it may be able to stand before the Face of the Cause of Causes.

The Twelfth Path is the Intelligence of Transparency, because it is that species of Magnificence called Chazchazit, [6] the place whence issues the vision of those seeing in apparitions. (That is the prophecies by seers in a vision.)

The Thirteenth Path is named the Uniting Intelligence, and is so called because it is itself the Essence of Glory. It is the Consummation of the Truth of individual spiritual things.

The Fourteenth Path is the Illuminating Intelligence and is so called because it is that *Chashmal* [7] which is the founder of the concealed and fundamental ideas of holiness and of their stages of preparation.

The Fifteenth Path is the Constituting Intelligence, so called because it constitutes the substance of creation in pure darkness, and men have spoken of these contemplations; it is that darkness spoken of in Scripture, Job xxxviii. 9, "and thick darkness a swaddling band for it."

The Sixteenth Path is the Triumphal or Eternal Intelligence, so called because it is the pleasure of the Glory, beyond which is no other Glory like to it, and it is called also the Paradise prepared for the Righteous.

The Seventeenth Path is the Disposing Intelligence, which provides Faith to the Righteous, and they are clothed with the Holy Spirit by it, and it is called the Foundation of Excellence in the state of higher things.

The Eighteenth Path is called the Intelligence or House of Influence (by the greatness of whose abundance the influx of good things upon created beings is increased), and from its midst the arcana and hidden senses are drawn forth, which dwell in its shade and which cling to it, from the Cause of all causes.

The Nineteenth Path is the Intelligence of the Secret of all the activities of the spiritual beings, and is so called because of the influence diffused by it from the most high and exalted sublime glory.

The Twentieth Path is the Intelligence of Will, and is so called because it is the means of preparation of all and each created being, and by this intelligence the existence of the Primordial Wisdom becomes known.

The Twenty-first Path is the Intelligence of Conciliation and Reward, and is so called because it receives the divine influence which flows into it from its benediction upon all and each existence.

The Twenty-second Path is the Faithful Intelligence, and is so called because by it spiritual virtues are increased, and all dwellers on earth are nearly under its shadow.

The Twenty-third Path is the Stable Intelligence, and it is so called because it has the virtue of consistency among all numerations.

The Twenty-fourth Path is the Imaginative Intelligence, and it is so called because it gives a likeness to all the similitudes which are created in like manner similar to its harmonious elegancies.

The Twenty-fifth Path is the Intelligence of Probation, or Temptation, and is so called because it is the primary temptation, by which the Creator trieth all righteous persons.

The Twenty-sixth Path is called the Renewing Intelligence, because the Holy God renews by it all the changing things which are renewed by the creation of the world.

The Twenty-seventh Path is the Active or Exciting Intelligence, and it is so called because through it every existent being receives its spirit and motion.

The Twenty-eighth Path is called the Natural Intelligence; by it is completed and perfected the nature of all that exists beneath the Sun.

(This Path is omitted by Rittangelius: I presume by inadvertence.)

The Twenty-ninth Path is the Corporeal Intelligence, so called because it forms every body which is formed in all the worlds, and the reproduction of them.

The Thirtieth Path is the Collective Intelligence, and Astrologers deduce from it the judgment of the Stars and celestial signs, and perfect their science, according to the rules of the motions of the stars.

The Thirty-first Path is the Perpetual Intelligence; but why is it so called? Because it regulates the motions of the Sun and Moon in their proper order, each in an orbit convenient for it.

The Thirty-second Path is the Administrative Intelligence, and it is so called because it directs and associates the motions of the seven planets, directing all of them in their own proper courses.

NOTES TO THE SEPHER YETZIRAH

It is of considerable importance to a clear understanding of this Occult treatise that the whole work be read through before comment is made, so that the general idea of the several chapters may become in the mind one concrete whole. A separate consideration of the several parts should follow this general grasp of the subject, else much confusion may result.

This hook may be considered to he an Allegorical Parallel between the Idealism of Numbers and Letters and the various parts of the Universe, and it sheds much light on many mystic forms and ceremonies yet extant, notably upon Freemasonry, the Tarot, and the later Kabalah, and is a great aid to the comprehension of the Astro-Theosophic schemes of the Rosicrucians. To obtain the full value of this Treatise, it should he studied hand in hand with Hermetic attributions, the "Isiac Tablet," and with a complete set of the designs, symbols and allocation of the Trump cards of the Tarot pack, for which see my translation of *The Sanctum Regnum of the Tarot*, by Eliphas Levi.

Note that the oldest MSS. copies of the "Sepher Yetzirah" have no vowel points: the latest editions have them. The system of points in writing Hebrew was not perfected until the seventh century, and even then was not in constant use. Ginsburg asserts that the system of vowel pointing was invented by a Rabbi Mocha in Palestine about A.D. 570, who designed it to assist his pupils. But Isaac Myer states that there are undoubted traces of pointing in

Hebrew MSS. of the second century. According to A. E. Waite there is no extant Hebrew MSS. with the vowel points older than the tenth century.

The words "Sepher Yetzirah" are written in Hebrew from right to left, SPR YTzYRH, Samech Peh Resh, Yod Tzaddi Yod Resh Heh; modes of transliteration vary with different authors. Yod is variously written in English letters as I, Y, or J, or sometimes Ie. Tzaddi is property Tz; but some write Z only, which is misleading because the Hebrew has also a true Z, Zain.

CHAPTER I

The twelve sections of this chapter introduce this philosophic disquisition upon the Formation and Development of the Universe. Having specified the subdivision of the letters into three classes, the Triad, the Heptad, and the Dodecad, these are put aside for the time; and the Decad mainly considered as specially associated with the idea of Number, and as obviously composed of the Tetrad and the Hexad.

1. *Thirty-two.* This is the number of the Paths or Ways of Wisdom, which are added as a supplement. 32 is written in Hebrew by LB, Lamed and Beth, and these are the last and first letters of the Pentateuch. The number 32 is obtained thus--$2 \times 2 \times 2 \times 2 \times 2 = 32$. Laib, LB as a Hebrew word, means the Heart of Man.

Paths. The word here is NTIBUT, netibuth; NTIB meant primarily a pathway, or foot-made track; but is here used symbolically in the same sense as the Christian uses the word, *way*--the way of life: other meanings are--stage, power, form, effect; and later, a doctrinal formula, in Kabalistic writings.

2. *Jah.* This divine name is found in Psalm lxviii. 4; it is translated into Greek as *kurios*, and into Latin as *dominus*, and commonly into the English word, *Lord*: it is really the first half of the word IHVH or Jehovah, or the Yahveh of modern scholars.

3. *Jehovah Tzabaoth*. This divine name is printed in English Bibles as Jehovah Sabaoth, or as "Lord of hosts" as in Psalm xxiv. 10. TzBA is an *army*.

4. *God of Israel*. Here the word God is ALHI, which in unpointed Hebrew might be God, or Gods, or My God.

5. *The Elohim of the Living*. The words are ALHIM ChIIM. Alhim, often written in English letters as Elohim, or by Godftey Higgins as Aleim, seems to be a masculine plural of the feminine form Eloah, ALH, of the divine masculine name EL, AL; this is commonly translated God, and means strong, mighty, supreme. Chiim is the plural of Chi--*living*, or *life*. ChIH is *a living animal*, and so is ChIVA. ChII is also *life*. Frey in his dictionary gives ChIIM as the plural word *lives*, or vitae. The true adjective for *living* is ChIA. Elohim Chiim, then, apart from Jewish or Christian preconception, is "the living Gods," or "the Gods of the lives, *i.e.,* living ones." Rittangelius gives Dii viventes, "The living Gods," both words in the plural. Pistorius omits both words. Postellus, the orthodox, gives Deus Vivus. The Elohim are the Seven Forces, proceeding from the One Divine, which control the "terra viventium," the manifested world of life.

6. *God*. In this case we have the simple form AL, EL.

7. *Sepharim*. SPRIM, the plural masculine of SPR, commonly translated *book* or *letter*: the meaning here is plainly "forms of expression."

8. *Numbers, Letters and Sounds*. The three Hebrew words here given are, in unpointed Hebrew, SPR, SPR and SIPUR. Some late editors, to cover the difficulty of this passage, have given SPR, SPUR, SIPR, pointing them to read Separ, Seepur, Saypar.

The sense of the whole volume appears to need their translation as Numbers, Letters and Sounds. Pistorius gave "Scriptis, numeratis, pronunciatis." Postellus gave "Numerans, numerus, numeratus," thus losing the contrasted meanings; and so did Rittangelius, who gave "Numero, numerante, numerato."

9. *The Ineffable Sephiroth.* The words are SPIRUT BLIMH, Sephiruth Belimah. The simplest translation is "the voices from nothing." The Ten Sephiruth of the Kabalah are the "Ten Primary Emanations from the Divine Source," which are the primal forces leading to all manifestation upon every plane in succession. Buxtorf gives for Sephiruth--predicationes logicae. The word seems to me clearly allied to the Latin spiritus--spirit, soul, wind; and is used by Quintilian as a sound, or noise. The meaning of *Belimah* is more doubtful. Rittangelius always gives "praeter illud ineffabile." Pistorius gives "praeter ineffabile." Postellus evades the difficulty and simply puts the word Belimah into his Latin translation. In Frey's Hebrew Dictionary BLIMH is translated as *nothing*, without any other suggestion; BLI is "not," MR is "anything." In Kabalistic writings the Sephiruth, the Divine Voices and Powers, are called "ineffbilis," not to be spoken of, from their sacred nature.

10. The classification of the Hebrew letters into a Triad, Heptad and Dodecad, runs through the whole philosophy of the Kabalah. Many ancient authors added intentional blinds, suds as forming the Triad of A.M.T., Ameth, truth; and of AMN, Amen.

11. The Two Covenants, by the Word or Spirit, and by the Flesh, made by Jehovah with Abraham, Genesis xvii. The Covenant of Circumcision was to be an outward and visible sign of the Divine promise made to Ahraham and his offspring. The Hebrew word for circumcision is Mulah, MULH: note that MLH is also synonymous with DBR, dabar,--verbum or word.

12. Rittangelius gives "replace the formative power upon his throne." Postellus gives restore the device to its place."

13. *Abyss*; the word is OUMQ for OMQ, a depth, vastness, or valley.

14. My Hermetic rituals explained this Yetziratic attribution.

15. *The Lord the only God.* The words are ADUN IChID AL, or "Adonai (as commonly written) the only El."

16. *Seat.* The word is MOUN, dwelling, habitation, or throne.

17. *Lightning flash.* In the early edition the words "like scintillating flame" are used: the Hebrew word is BRQ. Many Kabalists have shown how the Ten Sephiroth are symbolised by the zig-zag lightning flash.

18. *God*; the Divine name here is Jehovah.

19. The text gives only RTzUAV ShUB--"currendo et redeundo," but the commentators have generally considered this to be a quotation from Ezekiel i. 14, referred to H ChIVT, the living creatures, kerubic forms.

20. The Spirit of the Gods of the Living. RUCh ALHIM ChIIIM; or as R. gives it, "spiritus Deorum Viventium." Orthodoxy would translate these words "The spirit of the living God."

21. AL ChI H OULMIM; "the Living God of Ages"; here the word God really is in the singular.

22. The Voice, Spirit and Word are QUL, RUCh, DBR. A very notable Hebrew expression of Divinatory intuition was BATh QUL, the Daughter of the Voice.

23. Formless and Void. THU and BHU; these two words occur in Genesis i. 2, and are translated "waste and void."

24. Note the order in which the primordial elements were produced. First, Spirit (query Akasa, Ether); then Air, Vayu; then Water, Apas, which condenses into solid elementary Earth, Prithivi; and lastly from the Water He formed Fire.

25. The first name is often written Ophanim, the letters are AUPNIM; in the Vision of Ezekiel i. 16, the word occurs and is translated "Wheels." ShRPIM are the mysterious beings of Isaiah vi. 2; the word otherwise is translated *Serpent*, and in Numbers xxi. 6, as "fiery serpents": also in verse 8 as "fiery serpent" when Jehovah said "Make thee a fiery serpent and set it upon a pole."

Kerubim. The Hebrew words arc ChIVTh H QDSh, holy animals: I have ventured to put Kerubim, as the title of the other Biblical form of Holy mysterious animal, as given in 1 Kings vi. 23 and Exodus xxv. 18, and indeed Genesis iii. 24. Bible dictionaries generally give the word as Cherubim, but in Hebrew the initial letter is always K and not Ch.

26. Three. In the first edition I overlooked this word *three*; and putting *and* for *as*, made four classes of serving beings.

27. This is verse 4 of Psalm civ.

28. Here follow the permutations of the name IHV, which is the Tetragrammaton--Jehovah, without the second or final Heh: IHV is a Tri-grammaton, and is more suitable to the third or Yetziratic plane. HVI is the imperative form of the verb *to be*, meaning *be thou*; HIV is the infinitive; and VIH is future. In IHV note that Yod corresponds to the Father; Heh to Binah, the Supernal Mother; and Vau to the Microprosopus--Son.

29. Note the subdivision of the Decad into the Tetrad--four elements; and the Hexad--six dimensions of space.

CHAPTER II

This chapter consists of philosophic remarks on the twenty-two sounds and letters of the Hebrew alphabet, and hence connected with the air by speech, and it points out the uses of those letters to form words--the signs of ideas, and the symbols of material substances.

30. Soul; the word is NPSh, which is commonly translated soul, meaning the living personality of man, animal or existing thing: it corresponds almost to the Theosophic Prana plus the stimulus of Kama.

31. This is the modern classification of the letters into guttural, palatal, lingual, dental and labial sounds.

32. The 231 Gates. The number 242 is obtained by adding together all the numbers from 1 to 22. The Hebrew letters can he placed in pairs in 242 different positions: thus ab, ag, ad, up to at; then ba, bb, bg, bd, up to bt, and so on to ts, tt: this is in direct order only, without reversal. For the reason why eleven are deducted, and the number 231 specified, see the Table and Note 15 in the edition of Postellus.

33. Non-existent; the word is AIN, nothingness. Ain precedes Ain Suph, boundlessness; and Ain Suph Aur, Boundless Light.

34. Body; the word is GUP, usually applied to the animal material body, but here means "one whole."

CHAPTER III

This chapter is especially concerned with the essence of the Triad, as represented by the Three Mothers, Aleph, Mem, and Shin. Their development in three directions is pointed out, namely in the Macrocosm or Universe; in the Year or in Time; and in the Microcosm or Man.

35. The importance of equilibrium is constantly reiterated in the Kabalah. The "Siphra Dtzeniouta," or "Book of Mystery," opens with a reference to this Equilibrium as a fundamental necessity of stable existence.

36. Heavens. The Hebrew word Heshamaim HShMIM, has in it the element of Aesh, fire, and Mim, water; and also Shem, name; The Name is IHVH, attributed to the elements. ShMA is in Chaldee a name for the Trinity (Parkhurst). ShMSh is the Sun, and Light, and a type of Christ, the Sun of Righteousness. Malachi iv. 2.

37. Were produced. The Hebrew word BRA, is the root. Three Hebrew words are used in the Bible to represent the idea of making, producing or creating.

BRIAH, Briah, giving shape, Genesis i. 1.

OShIH, Ashiah, completing, Genesis i. 31.

ITzIRH, Yetzirah, forming, Genesis ii. 7.

To these the Kabalists add the word ATzLH, with the meaning of "producing something manifest from the unmanifested."

Emanation.	Shin.	Aleph.	Mem.
Macrocosm.	Primal Fire.	Spirit.	Primal Water.
Universe.	Heavens.	Atmosphere.	The Earth.
Elements.	Terrestrial Fire.	Air.	Water.
Man.	Head.	Chest.	Belly.
Year.	Heat.	Temperate.	Cold.

CHAPTER IV

This is the special chapter of the Heptad, the powers and properties of the Seven. Here again we have the threefold attribution of the numbers and letters to the Universe, to the Year, and to Man. The supplemental paragraphs have been printed in modern form by Kalisch; they identify the several letters of the Heptad more definitely with the planets, days of the week, human attributes and organs of the senses.

39. These numbers have been a source of difference between the editors and copyists, hardly any two editors concurring. I have given the numbers arising from continual multiplication of the product by each succeeding unit from one to seven. 2x1=2, 2x3=6, 6x4=24, 24x5=120, 120x6=720, 720x7=5040.

40. In associating the particular letters to each planet the learned Jesuit Athanasius Kircher allots Beth to the Sun, Gimel to Venus, Daleth to Mercury, Kaph to Luna, Peh to Saturn, Resh to Jupiter, and Tau to Mars. Kalisch in the supplementary paragraphs gives a different attribution; both are wrong, according to clairvoyant investigation. Consult the Tarot symbolism given by Court de Gebelin, Eliphas Levi, and my notes to the *Isiaic Tablet of Bembo*. The true attribution is probably not anywhere printed. The planet names here given are Chaldee words.

41. The Seven Heavens and the Seven Earths are printed with errors, and I believe intentional mistakes, in many occult ancient books. Some Hermetic MSS. have the correct names and spelling.

42. On the further attribution of these Seven letters, note that Postellus gives: Vita--mors, Pax--afflictio, Sapientia--stultitia, Divitiae (Opus)--paupertas, Gratia--opprobrium, Proles--sterilitas, Imperium--servitus. Pistorius gives: Vita--mors, Pax--bellum, Scientia--ignorantia, Divitiae--paupertas, Gratia--abominatio, Semen (Proles)--sterilitas, Imperium (Dominatio)--servitus.

CHAPTER V

This chapter is specially concerned with the Dodecad; the number twelve is itself pointed out, and the characters of its component units, once more in the three zones of the universe, year and man; the last paragraph gives a recapitulation of the whole number of letters: the Supplement gives a form of allotment of the several letters.

43. It is necessary to avoid confusion between these letters; different authors translate them in different manners. Heh or Hé not be confused with Cheth, or Heth, Ch. Teth, Th also must be kept distinct from the final letter Tau, T, which is one of the double letters; the semi-English pronunciation of these two letters is much confused, each is at times both t and th; Yod is either I, Y, or J; Samech is simple S, and must not be confused with Shin, Sh, one of the mother letters; Oin is often written in English Hebrew grammars as Ayin, and Sometimes as Gnain; Tzaddi must not be confused with Zain, Z; and lastly Qoph, Q, is very often replaced by K, which is hardly defensible as there is a true K in addition.

44. Postellus gives *suspicion* and Pistorius, *mind*.

45. These letters are the initials of the 12 Zodiacal signs in Hebrew nomenclature. They are:

| Teth | Telah | | Aries | Mem | | Maznim | Libra |
| Shin | Shor | | Taurus | Oin | | Oqereb | Scorpio |

Tau	Thaumim	Gemini	Qoph	Qesheth	Sagittarius
Samech	Sartan	Cancer	Gimel	Gedi	Capricornus
Aleph	Aryeh	Leo	Daleth	Dali	Aquarius
Beth	Bethuleh	Virgo	Daleth	Dagim	Pisces

46. The month Nisan begins about March 29th. Yiar is also written Iyar, and Aiar: the Hebrew letters are AIIR.

47. The list of organs varies. All agree in two hands, two feet, two kidneys, liver, gall and spleen. Postellus then gives, intestina, vesica, arteriae," the intestines, bladder, and arteries; Rittangelius gives the same. Pistorius gives, "colon, coagulum (spleen) et ventriculus," colon--the large intestine, coagulum and stomach. The chief difficulty is with the Hebrew word MSS, which is allied to two different roots, one meaning *private, concealed, hidden*; and the other meaning *liquefied*.

48. The Elohim--Divine powers--not IHVH the Tetragrammaton.

CHAPTER VI

This chapter is a resumé of the preceding five; it calls the universe and mankind to witness to the truth of the scheme of distribution of the powers of the numbers among created forms, and concludes with the narration that this philosophy was revealed by the Divine to Abraham, who received and faithfully accepted it, as a form of Wisdom under a Covenant.

49. The Dragon, TLI, Theli. The Hebrew letters amount in numeration to 440, that is 400, 30 and 10. The best opinion is that Tali or Theli refers to the 12 Zodiacal constellations along the great circle of the Ecliptic; where it ends there it begins again, and so the ancient occultists drew the Dragon with its tail in its mouth. Some have thought that Tali referred to the constellation Draco, which meanders across the Northern polar sky; others have referred it to the Milky Way; others to an imaginary line joining Caput to Cauda Draconis, the upper and lower nodes of the Moon. Adolphe Franck says that Theli is an Arabic word.

50. Happiness, or a good end, or simply good, TUBH.

51. Misery, or an evil end, or simply evil, ROH.

52. This Hebrew version omits the allotment of the remaining six. Mayer gives the paragraph thus:--The triad of amity is the heart and the two ears; the triad of enmity is the liver, gall, and the tongue; the three life-givers are the two nostrils and the spleen;

the three death-dealing ones are the mouth and the two lower openings of the body.

53. God. In this case the name is AL, EL.

54. This last paragraph is generally considered to be less ancient than the remainder of the treatise, and by another author.

55. The Lord most high. OLIU ADUN. Adun or Adon, or Adonai, ADNI, are commonly translated Lord; Eliun, OLIUN, is the more usual form of "the most high one."

56. Him. Rittangelius gives "credidit in Tetragrammaton," but this word is not in the Hebrew.

57. Tongue. The verbal covenant.

58. Speech. The Hebrew has "upon his tongue."

59. The Hebrew version of Rabbi Judah Ha Levi concludes with the phrase, "and said of him, Before I formed thee in the belly, I knew thee." Rabbi Luria gives the Hebrew version which I have translated. Postellus gives: "He drew him into the water, He rose up in spirit, He inflamed him in seven suitable forms with twelve signs." Mayer gives: "Er zog sie mit Wasser, zundet sie an mit Feuer; erregte sie mit Geist; verbannte sie mit sieben, goss sie aus mit den zwolf Gestirnen." "He drew them with water, He kindled them with fire, He moved them with spirit, distributed them with seven, and sent them forth with twelve."

NOTES TO THE THIRTY-TWO PATHS OF WISDOM

1. The Highest Crown is Kether, the First Sephira, the first emanation from the Ain Suph Aur, the Limit-less Light.

2. Binah, or Understanding, is the Third Sephira.

3. Chokmah, Wisdom, is the Second Sephira.

4. Gedulah is a synonym of Chesed, Mercy, the Fourth Sephira.

5. Metatron, the Intelligence of the First Sephira, and the reputed guide of Moses.

6. This word is from ChZCh, a seer, seership. Chazuth is a vision.

7. This word means "scintillating flame."

The "Thirty-two Paths of Wisdom" refer to the Ten Sephiroth and the Twenty-two letters, each supplying a type of divine power and attributes. In my Introduction to the Kabalah will be found a diagram showing how the Paths from Eleven to Thirty-two connect the several Sephiroth, and are deemed to transmit the divine influence. Some teachers of Occult Science also allot the Twenty-two Trumps of the Tarot Cards to the twenty-two Paths.

GRIMOIRIUM VERUM

GRIMOIRIUM VERUM

OR

THE TRUE GRIMOIRE

THE MOST APPROVED KEYS OF SOLOMON THE HEBREW RABBI WHEREIN THE MOST HIDDEN SECRETS, BOTH NATURAL AND SUPERNATURAL ARE IMMEDIATELY EXHIBITED.

Modo operator per necessaria et contenta facit scia tamen oportit Daemonum potentia dum taxat per agantur.

TRANSLATED FROM THE HEBREW by PLAINGIERE JESUIT DOMINICAINE. with a Curious collection of Rare and Astounding Magical Secrets.
EDITED, WITH A PREFACE BY JAMES BANNER, Gent.

ORIGINALLY PUBLISHED BY ALIBECK THE ÆGYPTIAN at Memphis 1517.

INTRODUCTION

In the first part is contained various dispositions of characters, by which powers the spirits or, rather, the devils are invoked, to make them come when you will, each according to his power, and to bring whatever is asked: and that without any discomfort, providing also that they are content on their part; for this sort of creature does not give anything for nothing. In the first part is taught the means of calling forth the Elemental Spirits of the Air, Earth, Sea or of the Infernus, according to their affinities.

In the second part are expressed the secrets, both Natural and Supernatural which operate by the power of the Dmons. You will find the manner to make use of them, and all without deceit.

In the third part is the Key to the Work, with the manner of using it. But, before starting this, it will be necessary to be instructed in the following: There are three powers, which are Lucifer, Beelzebuth and Astaroth. You must engrave their Characters in the correct manner and at the appropriate hours. Believe me, all this is of consequence, nothing is to be forgotten.

THE FIRST BOOK

CONCERNING THE CHARACTERS OF THE DAEMONS

You must carry the aforesaid character with you. If you are male, in the right pocket, and it is to be written in your own blood, or that of a sea-turtle. You put at the two half-circles the first letter of your name and surname. And if you wish more, you may draw the character on an emerald or ruby, for they have a sympathy for the spirits, especially those of the Sun, who are the most knowledgeable, and are better than the others. If you are a female, carry the character on the left side, between the breasts, like a Reliquary; and always observing, as much as the other sex, to write or have engraved the character on the day and in the hour of Mars. Obey the spirits in this, that they may obey thee.

The spirits who are powerful and exalted, serve only their confidants and intimate friends, by the pact made or to be made according to certain characters at the will of Singambuth or of his Secretary. Aabidandes, of whom we will give you information, is the perfect acquaintance to call, conjure and constrain, as you will see in the Key, where you will be given a method of making a pact with the spirits.

OF THE NATURE OF PACTS

There are only two kinds of pact, the tacit and the apparent [or explicit]. You will know the one from the other, if you read this little book. Know, however, that there are many kinds of spirits, some attractive and others not attractive.

It is when you make a pact with a spirit, and have to give the spirit something which belongs to you, that you have to be on your guard.

THE KINDS OF SPIRITS

In regard to spirits, there are the superior and the inferior. Names of the superiors are: Lucifer, Beelzebuth, Astaroth. The inferiors of Lucifer are in Europe and Asia, and obey him. Beelzebuth lives in Africa, and Astaroth inhabits America.

Of these, each of them has two who order their subjects all that which the Emperor has resolved to do in all the world, and vice-versa.

THE VISIBLE APPEARANCE OF SPIRITS

Spirits do not always appear in the same shape. This is because they are not themselves of matter or form, and have to find a body to appear in, and one suitable to their intended manifestation and appearance.

Lucifer appears in the form and figure of a fair boy. When angry, he seems red. There is nothing monstrous about him.

Beelzebuth appears sometimes in monstrous forms, sometimes like a giant cow, at times like a he-goat, with a long tail. When angry, he vomits fire.

Astaroth appears black, in human shape.

Here are three characters of Lucifer, outside his circle:

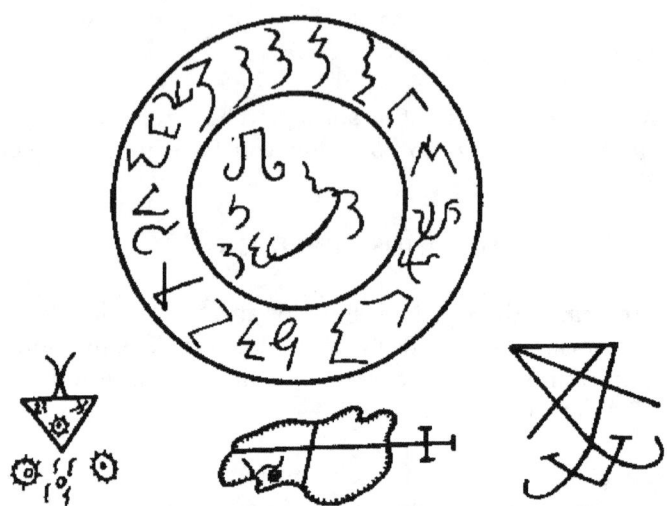

The following are those of Beelzebuth and Astaroth placed outside their circles:

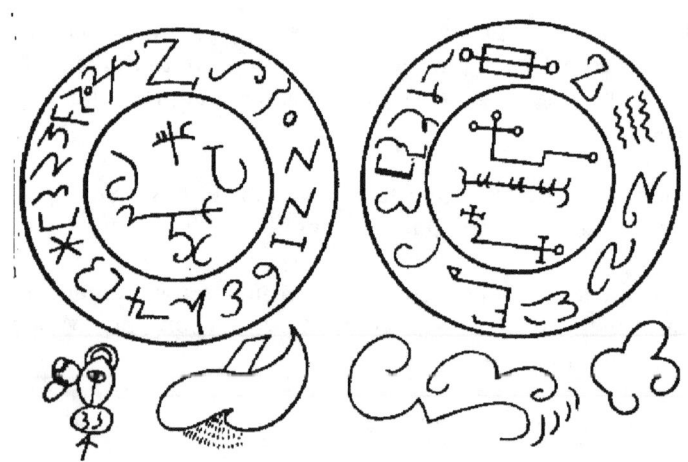

TO INVOKE THE SPIRITS

It is only necessary, when you desire to invoke them, to call them by their characters, which they themselves have given. And when you wish to invoke them, call them to serve you, in the manner taught in the Third Part.

DESCENDING TO THE INFERIORS

Lucifer has two demons under him: Satanackia and Agalierap. Those of Beelzebuth are Tarchimache and Fleruty. The characters of Satanackia and Fleruty are:

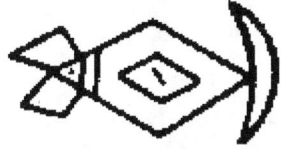   

The two inferiors of Astaroth are Sagatana and Nesbiros, and their characters are:

There are yet other dmons, apart from these, who are under Duke Syrach. There are eighteen of these, and their names are:

I. Clauneck

II. Musisin

III. Bechaud

IV. Frimost

V. Klepoth

VI. Khil

VII. Mersilde

VIII. Clisthert

IX. Sirchade

X. Segal

XI. Hicpacth

XII. Humots

XIII. Frucissiere

XIV. Guland

XV. Surgat

XVI. Morail

XVII. Frutimiere

XVIII. Huictiigaras

These are the characters of fifteen inferior spirits:

BUCON

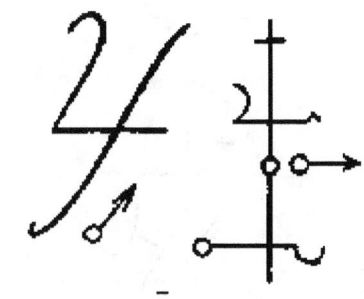

CLISTHERT

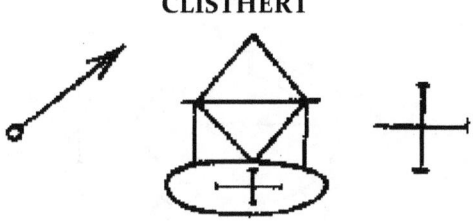

FRUCISSIERE

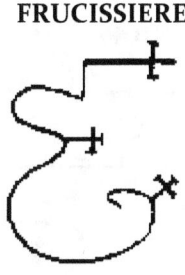

GULAND

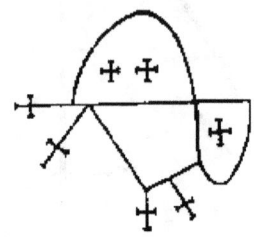

MORAIL

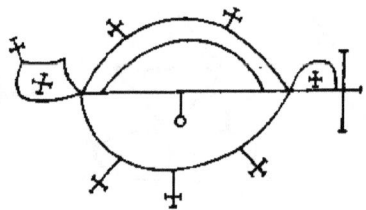

HICPACTH

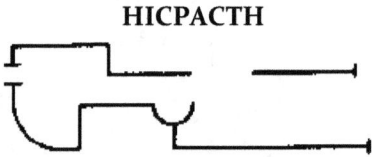

FRUTIMIERE

HUICTIIGARAS

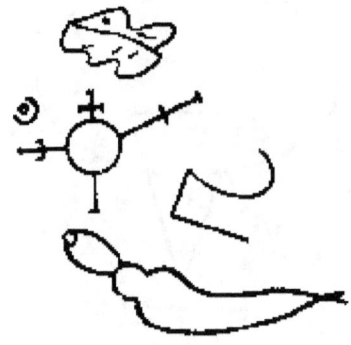

HUMOTS

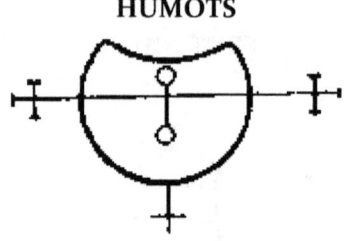

KHIL

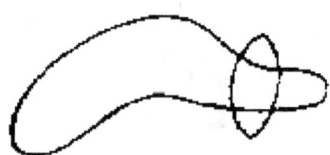

MERSILDE

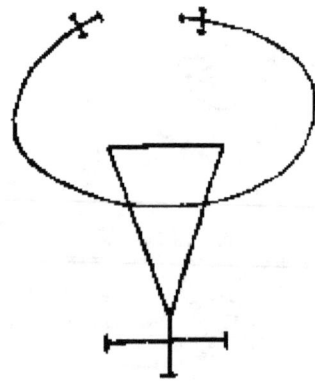

MINOSON

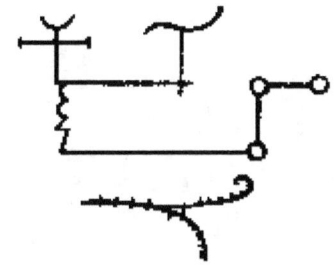

SEGAL

SIRCHADE

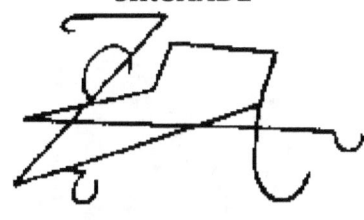

SURGAT

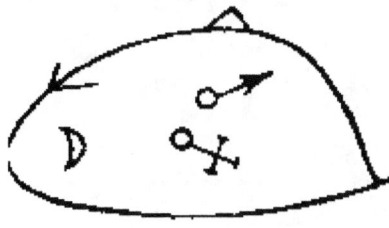

THE SECOND BOOK

THE SECOND BOOK

AGLA * ADONAY * JEHOVA

There are other daemons, but as they have no power, we shall not speak of them. The powers of the eighteen above-mentioned ones are these:

CLAUNECK has power over riches, can cause treasures to be found. He can give great riches to he who makes a pact with him, for he is much loved by Lucifer. It is he who causes money to be brought.

MUSISIN has power over great lords, teaches all that happens in the Republics, and Ôthe affairs of the AlliesÕ.

FRIMOST has power over women and girls, and will help you to obtain their use.

KLEPOTH makes you see all sorts of dreams and visions.

KHIL makes great earthquakes.

MERSILDE has the power to transport anyone in an instant, anywhere.

CLISTHERT allows you to have day or night, whichever you wish, when you desire either.

SIRCHADE makes you see all sorts of natural and supernatural animals.

HICPACTH will bring you a person in an instant, though he be far away.

HUMOTS can bring you any book you desire.

SEGAL will cause all sorts of prodigies to appear.

FRUCISSIRE revives the dead.

GULAND causes all illnesses.

SURGAT opens every kind of lock.

MORAIL can make anything invisible.

FRUTIMIRE prepares all kinds of feasts for you.

HUICTIIGARAS causes sleep in the case of some, and insomnia in others.

Under Satanachia and Sataniciae are fourty-five [or, according to other versions, fifty-four] daemons. Four of these, the chiefs, are Sergutthy, Heramael, Trimasael and Sustugriel. The others are of no great consequence.

These spirits are of great advantage, and they work well and speedily, in the case that they are pleased with the operator.

Sergutthy has power over maidens and wives, when things are favorable.

Heramael teaches the art of healing, including the complete knowledge of any illness and its cure, He also makes known the virtues of plants, where they are to be found, when to pluck them, and their making into a complete cure.

Trimasael teaches chemistry and all means of conjuring of the nature of deceit or sleight-of-hand. He also teaches the secret of making the Powder of Projection, by means of which the base metals may be turned into gold or silver.

Sustugriel teaches the art of magic. He gives familiar spirits that can be used for all purposes, and he also gives mandragores.

Agalierept and Tarihimal are the rulers of Elelogap, who in turn governs matters connected with water.

Nebirots rules Hael and Surgulath. The former (Hael) enables anyone to speak in any language he will, and also teches the means whereby any type of letter may be written. He is also able to teach those things which are most secret and completely hidden.

Sergulath gives every means of speculation. In addition, he instructs as to the methods of breaking the ranks and strategy of opponents. Subject to these are the eight most powerful subordinates:

I. PROCULO, who can cause a person to sleep for forty-eight hours, with the knowledge of the spheres of sleep.

II. HARISTUM, who can cause anyone to pass through fire without being touched by it.

III. BRULEFER, who causes a person to be beloved of women.

IV. PENTAGNONY, who gives the two benefits of attaining invisibility and the love of great lords.

V. AGLASIS, who can carry anyone or anything anywhere in the world.

VI. SIDRAGOSAM, causes any girl to dance in the nude.

VII. MINOSON, is able to make anyone win at any game.

VIII. BUCON, can cause hate and spiteful jealousy between members of the opposite sexes.

THE THIRD BOOK

THE THIRD BOOK

THE INVOCATION

This is the Invocation:

HELOY + TAU + VARAF + PANTHON + HOMNORCUM + ELEMIATH + SERUGEATH + AGLA + ON + TETRAGRAMMATON + CASILY.

This Invocation is to be made on virgin parchment, with the characters of the Dmon upon it, which causes the intermediary Scirlin to come. For from this depend all the others, and it can constrain them to appear in spite of themselves, as he has the power of Emperor.

ORISON: PREPARATION

Lord God Adonay, who hast made man in Thine own image and resemblance out of nothing! I, poor sinner that I am, beg Thee to deign bless and sanctify this water, so that it may be healthy for my body and my soul, and that all foolishness should depart from it.

Lord God, all-powerful and ineffable, and who led Thy people out of the land of Ægypt, and has enabled them to cross the Red Sea with dry feet! Accord me this, that I may be purified by this water of all my sins, so that I may appear innocent before Thee! Amen.

When the operator has thus purified himself, he is to set about the making of the Instruments of the Art.

OF THE MAGICAL KNIFE

It is necessary to have a knife or lancet, of new steel, made on the day and hour of Jupiter with the Moon crescent. If it cannot be made, it may be bought, but this must be done at the time, as above.

Having achieved this, you will say the Orison or Conjuration following, which will serve for the knife and lancet.

CONJURATION OF THE INSTRUMENT

I conjure thee, O form of the Instrument, by the authority of our Father God Almighty, by the virtues of Heaven and by the Stars, by the virtue of the Angels, and by the virtue of the Elements, by the virtues of the stones and herbs, and of snow-storms, winds and thunder: that thou now obtain all the necessary power into thyself for the pefectioning of the achievement of those things in which we are at present concerned! And this without deception, untruth, or anything of that nature whatsoever, by God the Creator of the Sun of Angels! Amen.

Then we recite the Seven Psalms, and afterwards the following words:

Dalmaley lamekh cadat pancia velous merro lamideck caldurech anereton mitraton: Most Pure Angels, be the guardians of these instruments, they are needed for many things.

THE SACRIFICIAL KNIFE

On the day of Mars [Tuesday] at the New Moon, make a knife of new steel which is strong enough to cut the neck of a kid with one blow, and make a handle of wood on the same day and in the same hour, and with an engraver you engrave on the handle these characters:

Then asperge and fumigate it, and you have prepared an instrument for service when and where you wish.

THE MANNER OF ASPERGING & FUMIGATION

First, there is the Orison which is needful on asperging, and it is thus recited:

In the name of the immortal God, asperge [N] and clean you of all foolishness and all deceit, and you will be whiter than snow. Amen.

Then pour as the aspersion blessed water thereon, saying:

In the name of the Father + and of the Son + and of the Holy + Ghost, Amen.

These aspersions are necessary for every item of equipment; so also is the fumigation which follows.

To fumigate, it is necessary to have a cruse, in which you place coal newly kindled with a new fire, and let it be well ablaze. On this you place aromatics, and when perfuming the article in question, say the following:

Angels of God, be our help, and may our work be accomplished by you. Zalay, Salmay, Dalmay, Angrecton, Ledrion, Amisor, Euchey, Or. Great Angels: And do thou also, O Adonay, come and give to this a virtue so that this creature may gain a shape, and by this let our work be accomplished. In the name of the Father + and of the Son + and of the Holy + Ghost, Amen.

Then recite the Seven Psalms which come after Judicum tuum Regida and Laudate Dominum omnes gentes.

OF THE VIRGIN PARCHMENT

Virgin parchment can be made in many ways. Generally it is made of the skin of a goat or a lamb, or other animal, which must be virgin.

After inscribing on the blade AGLA, and having fumigated it, the knife will serve you for all purposes.

Remember that when you make the Sacrifice in order to obtain the virgin parchment from the kid, all the instruments must be on the altar.

You make the baton [or Rod, staff] of the Art from Hazel wood that has never borne, and cut it with a single stoke on the day and in the hour of Mercury [Wednesday], at the Crescent Moon. And you engrave it with the needle, the pen or the lancet, in the following characters:

The seal and character of Frimost to be inscribed on the first Rod:

Then you make another baton of Hazel wood, which has never borne, and which is without seed, and cut it in the day and hour of the Sun [Sunday], and on this you engrave these characters:

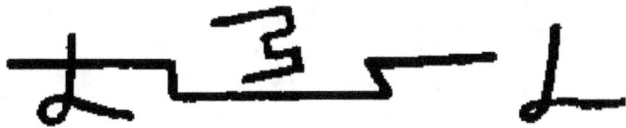

The seal and character of Klippoth is to be inscribed on the second Rod.

This having been done, you say over your baton the following Orison:

ORISON

Most wise, most powerful Adonay, deign to bless, sanctify and conserve this baton so that it may have the necessary virtue, O most holy Adonay, to whom be honor and glory for all time. Amen.

OF THE LANCET

It is necessary to have a new lancet, conjured and prepared like the knife and sickle. Make it in the day and hour of Mercury, at the Crescent Moon. Now follows the method of Making the Sacrifice of the Kid.

Take your goat and place it on a flat surface, so that the throat is uppermost, the better to cut it. Take your knife and cut the throat with a single stroke, while pronouncing the name of the Spirit you wish to invoke.

For example, you say:

I kill you in the name and in the honor of [N]. . .

This is to be well understood, and take care that you sever the throat at first, and do not take two strokes, but see that he dies at the first.

Then you skin him with the knife, and at the skinning make this Invocation:

INVOCATION

Adonay, Dalmay, Lauday, Tetragrammaton, Anereton, and all you, Holy Angels of God, come and be here, and deign to infuse into this skin the power that it may be correctly conserved, so that all that is written upon it may become perfected.

After the skinning, take well-ground salt, and strew this upon the skin, which has been stretched, and let the salt cover the skin well. Before you use the salt it must have the following Benediction said over it.

THE BENEDICTION OF THE SALT

I exorcise you, O creature of the Salt, by the God who is living, the God of all Gods, the Lord of all Lords, that all fantasies may leave you, and that you may be suitable for the virgin parchment.

When this is finished, let the skin with the salt upon it remain in the sun for a full day. Then obtain a glazed pottery jar, and write these characters around it with the Pen of the Art:

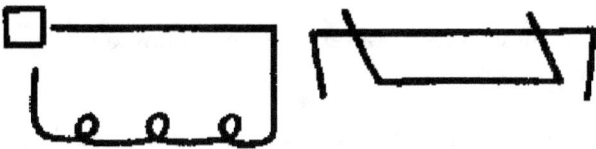

Get quicklime and slake this with exorcised water, and put these in the jar. When it is liquid place it in your goatskin, and leave it long enough for the hairs to peel off of themselves.

As soon as the hair is in such a condition as to come off with a touch, remove it from the jar and peel the hairs with a knife made from carved Hazel. The knife must have had these words said over it:

O holiest Adonay, put into this wood the power to cleanse this skin, through the holy name Agason, Amen.

The skin, when peeled, may be stretched over a piece of new wood, and stones are to be placed on the skin, so that they hold it down. These are to be stones from a river bank. Before placing the stones, say the following Orison over them.

THE ORISON OF THE STONES

O Adonay, most puissant and all-powerful Lord, allow that these stones may stretch this skin, and remove from them all wickedness, so that they may possess the required power. Amen.

OF THE ASPERSION OF THE WATER

All water used in these experiments must be asperged, by saying this over it:

Lord God, Father, all-powerful, my refuge and my life, help me, Holy Father, for I love you, God of Abraham, of Isaac, of Jacob, of the Archangels and Prophets, Creator of All. In humility, and, calling upon Thy holy Name, I supplicate that thou wilt agree to bless this water, so that it may sanctify our bodies and our souls, through Thee, most holy Adonay, Everlasting Ruler, Amen.

The skin is allowed to dry after this, and before quitting the spot, say over the parchment:

Je, Agla, Jod, Hoi, He, Emmanuel! Stand guard over this parchment, in order that no spectra may take charge of it!

When the skin is dry it may be removed from its wodden frame, blessed and fumigated, and then it is ready for use.

It is important that this must not be seen by any women, and more especially during certain times of theirs [i.e., during menstruation], otherwise it will lose its power. It must also be known that when you make and use this parchment, you must be clean, pur and chaste.

The operator is to say one Mass of the Nativity then, and all the instruments are to be on the altar.

OF ASPERSION

You take an asperser made with a bunch of mint, marjoram and rosemary which is secured by a thread which has been made by a virgin maiden.

The asperger is made in the day and hour of Mercury when the Moon is at its crescent.

OF THE PERFUMES

These are to be wood of aloes, incense and mace. As for the mace, this is all that you need for the circle, and over the perfumes is to be said the following Orison:

THE ORISON OF THE AROMATIC PERFUMES

Deign, O Lord, to sanctify the creature of this, in order that it may be a remedy for the human race, and that it may be a remedy for our souls and bodies, through the invoking of Thy holy Name! Agree that all creatures which may breathe in the vapor of this may have wealth of their bodies and souls: through the Lord who has fashioned the time eternal! Amen.

OF THE PEN OF THE ART

Take a new quill, and asperge and fumigate this in the same way as the other instruments, and when you are cutting its points, say:

Ababaloy, Samoy, Escavor, Adonay: I have from this quill driven out all illusions, so that it may hold within it with effectiveness the power needed for all those things which are used in the Art: for both the operations and the characters and conjurations. Amen.

OF THE INK-HORN

You buy a new Ink-horn on the day and in the hour of Mercury. At this time, also, these characters are [to be] inscribed upon it:

JOD HE VAU HE + METATRON + JOD + KADOS + ELOHIM SABAOTH.

Then newly-made ink is exorsized with this exorcism before being placed in the horn:

I exorcise you, Creature of this Ink, by the names Anston, Cerreton, Stimulator, Adonay, and by the Name of He who created all by one word, and who can achieve all, so that you shall assist me in my work, and so this work may be accomplished by my desire, and brought to a successful end through the aggreement of God, He who rules all things, and through all things, omnipresent and eternal. Amen.

Then the ink is to be blessed with this Blessing:

Lord God, Almighty, ruler over all and forever, Thou who dost cause to take place the greatest wonders in Thy creations, deign to grant the grace of Thy holy spirit through this ink. Bless it, and sanctify it, and impart to it a special power, that whatever we may say or do or desire may be accomplished: through Thee, Most Holy Prince, ADONAY. Amen.

THE PREPERATION OF THE OPERATOR

When the implements are ready, the operator must prepare himself. This is first done by this Preparatory Orison:

Lord God, ADONAY, who hast formed man in Thine image, I, the unworthy and sinful, beseech Thee to sanctify this water, to benefit my body and soul, cause me to be cleansed.

As he says this the operator is to wash his face and hands with the water that he is blessing.

NOTE: This water is to be used for washing the hands and feet, and know alsoÑand know and know againÑthat it is necessary and most necessary, to abstain three days from sin: and above all mortally, however much the human frailty may be, and especially guard your chastity.

During the three days, study the book and during this time, pray five times during the day and four times each night, with the following form:

Astrachios, Asach, Ascala, Abedumabal, Silat, Anabotas, Jesubilin, Scingin, Geneon, Domol: O Lord my God, Thou who art seated higher than the Heavens, Thou who art seated higher than the Heavens, Thou who seeth even unto the depths, I pray that Thou unto me the things which I have in my mind and that I may be successful in them: through Thee, O Great God, the Eternal and who reigns for ever and ever. Amen. [Shah gives a note of a variation: "Astrocio, Asath, a sacra Bedrimubal, Felut, Anabotos, Serabilem, Sergen, Gemen, Domos: . . ."]

All this having been done correctly, all that remains is to follow your invocations and draw your characters and you do as follows.

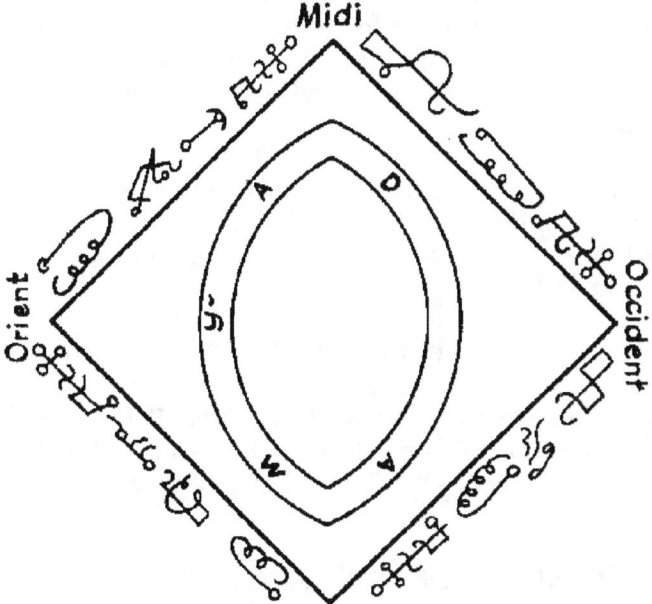

In the day and hour of Mars [Tuesday] the Moon being at the crescent, and at the first hour of the dayÑwhich is a quarter of an hour before sunriseÑyou will prepare a piece of virgin parchment, which shall contain all the characters and the invocations of the spirits which you wish to produce.

For example, in the said day and hour, you will attach to the small finger of the hand (which is the finger of Mercury) a thread spun by a virgin girl, and pierce the finger with the lancet of the Art, to get blood from it, with which you form your Scirlin character, as is given at the commencement of this book. Then write your invocation, which is that which follows.

INVOCATION TO SCIRLIN

HELON + TAUL + VARF + PAN + HEON + HOMONOREUM + CLEMIALH + SERUGEATH + AGLA + TETRAGRAMMATON + CASOLY.

You must write the first letter of your name where is the letter A [in the sign & character of Scirlin], and that of your surname where is the letter D. The spirit Aglassis, whose character it is, is very potent to render you service, and will cause you to have power over the other spirits.

Make above the Character of the Spirit that you desire to come, and burn incense in his honor. Then make the conjuration which is addressed to the spirit that you want to cause to appear, and burn incense in his honor.

CONJURATION FOR LUCIFER

Lucifer, Ouyar, Chameron, Aliseon, Mandousin, Premy, Oriet, Naydrus, Esmony, Eparinesont, Estiot, Dumosson, Danochar, Casmiel, Hayras, Fabelleronthou, Sodirno, Peatham, Come, Lucifer, Amen.

CONJURATION FOR BEELZEBUTH

Belzbuth, Lucifer, Madilon, Solymo, Saroy, Theu, Ameclo, Sagrael, Praredun, Adricanorom, Martino, Timo, Cameron, Phorsy, Metosite, Prumosy, Dumaso, Elivisa, Alphrois, Fubentroty, Come, Beelzebuth, Amen.

CONJURATION FOR ASTAROTH

Astaroth, Ador, Cameso, Valuerituf, Mareso, Lodir, Cadomir, Aluiel, Calniso, Tely, Plorim, Viordy, Cureviorbas, Cameron, Vesturiel, Vulnavij, Benez meus Calmiron, Noard, Nisa Chenibranbo Calevodium, Brazo Tabrasol, Come, Astaroth, Amen.

After having said seven times the conjuration addressed to superior spirits, you will see the spirit at once appear, to do whatever you desire.

NOTE
Dismissal of the Spirit.

When you have written the conjuration on the virgin parchment, and have seen the spirit, being satisfied, you can dismiss him by saying this:

Ite in pace ad loca vestra et pax sit inter vos redituri ad mecum vos invocavero, in nomine Patris + et Filii + et Spiritus Sancti + Amen.

[Go in peace unto your abode and let there be peace between you and I, and be ready to come to me when you are called, in the name of the Father + and the Son + and of the Holy Spirit + Amen]

CONJURATION FOR INFERIOR SPIRITS

OSURMY + DELMUSAN + ATALSLOYM + CHARUSIHOA + MELANY + LIAMINTHO + COLEHON + PARON + MADOIN + MERLOY + BULERATOR + DONMEDO + HONE + PELOYM + IBASIL + MEON + ALYMDRICTELS + PERSON + CRISOLSAY + LEMON SESSLE NIDAR HORIEL PEUNT + HALMON + ASOPHIEL + ILNOSTREON + BANIEL + VERMIAS + SLEVOR + NOELMA + DORSAMOT + LHAVALA + OMOR + FRAMGAM + BELDOR + DRAGIN + Come, N. . .

DISMISSAL OF THE INFERIOR SPIRIT

Go in peace, N., whence you came, peace be with you, and come every time I shall call you, in the name of the Father + and of the Son + and of the Holy Spirit + Amen.

Then you will burn the characters, because they will serve only once.

ANOTHER CONJURATION

I conjure thee, N., by the name of the Great Living God, Sovereign Creator of all things, that thou appear in human form, fair and aggreeable, without noise or inconvenience, to answer truthfully in all the interrogations that I shall make. I conjure thee to do this by the power of the Holy and Sacred Names.

ORISON OF THE SALAMANDERS

Immortal, eternal, ineffable and Holy Father of all things, who is carried by the revolving chariot unceasingly, of the worlds which continually revolve: dominator of the Etherian countries where there is raised the throne of Thy power: above which Thy redoubtable eyes see all, and Thy holy ears hear allÑaid Thy children whom Thou hast loved since the birth of the centuries: for thy golden and great and eternal majesty shines above the world, the sky and the stars, Thou art elevated above all, O sparkling fire, and Thou illuminatest Thyself by Thy splendor, and there go out from Thy essence untarnishable rays of light which nourish Thy infinite spirit. That infinite spirit produces all things, and makes the mighty treasure which cannot fail, to the creation which surrounds Thee, due to the numberless forms of which she bears, and which Thou hast filled at the start. From this spirit comes also the origin of those most holy kings who are around Thy throne, and who compose Thy court, O Universal Father!

O Unique One, O Father of happy mortals and immortals! Thou hast created in particular the powers which are marvellously like the eternal thought, and from Thy adorable essence. Thou hast established them over the angels, Thou hast created a third kind of sovereign in the elements. Our cintinual exercise is to worship Thy desires. We burn with the desire to possess Thee, O Father, O Mother, the most tender of Mothers! O wonderful example of feelings and tenderness of Mothers! O Son, the flower of all sons! O Form of all forms! Soul, Spirit, Harmony, and Name of all things, preserve us and we shall be blessed. Amen.

OF THE PENTACLE AND THE MANNER OF WORKING

I have put here the form of the Pentacle of Solomon so that you may make the arrangements, they being of great importance.

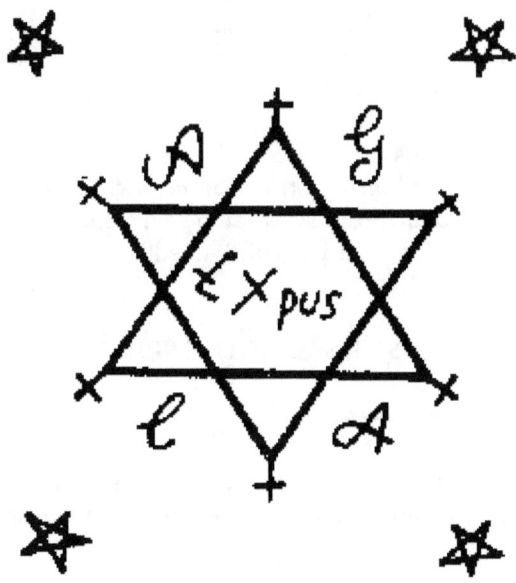

When you make your circle, before entering therein, it is to be perfumed with musk, amber, aloes wood and incense. And for the perfume which you will need for the invocations, that is incense alone.

It is to be observed that you need to have always a fire during invocations, and when you perfume, this will be in the name of the spirit that you would invoke. When you are placing the perfume on the fire, say all the time:

I burn this, N., in the name and to the honor of N.

It is to be remembered that you must hold the invocation in the left hand, and in the right a rod of elder, and a ladle and a knife are to be at your feet.

When all this is ready, stand inside the circle. If you have companions with you, they are to hold a hand one of the other. When inside, trace the form of the circle with the knife of the Art. Then pick up the wands, one after the other, reciting the Fiftieth Psalm. When the circle is complete, perfume and sprinkle it with holy water. Characters are to written at the four corners of the circle. There are generally four pentacles, one at each point of the compass; and the spirit is prohibited specifically from entering into the precints of the circle.

Then the invocations are to be repeated seven times. When the spirit appears, make him sign the character which you are holding in your hand, which promises that he will come whenever you may call him. Ask for what you think needed, and he will give it to you.

DISMISSAL OF THE SPIRIT

Let him go away in these words:

Ite in pace ad loca vestra et pax sit inter vos redituri ad mecum vos invocavero, in nomine Patris + et Filii + et Spiritus Sancti + Amen.

[Go in peace unto your abode and let there be peace between you and I, and be ready to come to me when you are called, in the name of the Father + and the Son + and of the Holy Spirit + Amen]

A RARE & SUPRISING MAGICAL SECRET

The manner of making the Mirror of Solomon, useful for all divinations.

In the name of the Lord, Amen. YE shall see in this mirror anything which you may desire. In the name of the Lord who is blessd, in the name of the Lord, Amen. Firstly, you shall abstain from all actions of the flesh, and also from any sin, whether in word or action, during the period of time laid down herein. Secondly, you must perform acts of good and piety. Thirdly, take a plate of finest steel, burnished and slightly curved, and with the blood of a white pigeon write upon it, at the four corners, these names: JEHOVA, ELOYM, METATRON, ADONAY.

Place the steel in a clean, white cloth. Look for the new Moon, in the first hour after the Sun has set, and when you see it, go to a window, look devoutly towards Heaven, and say:

O Eternal, O King Eternal! God Ineffable! Thou, who hast created all things for the love of men, and by a concealed decision for the wellbeing of man, deign Thou to look on me, N., who am Thy most unfit and unworthy Servant, and look upon this, which is my intention.

Deign to send unto me Thine Angel, Ana'l upon this same mirror; he does command and order his companionsÑwhom Thou hast formed, O Most Powerful Lord, who hast always been, who art, and who shall ever be, so that in Thy name they may work and act with equity, giving me knowledge in everything that I shall seek to know of them.

Now you are to throw down upon the burning embers a perfume. While you are doing this, say:

In this and with this, that I pour forth before Thy face, O God, my God, Thou who art blessd, Three in One, and in the state of exaltation most sublime, who sits above the Cherubim and Seraphim, who will judge the earth by fire, hear me!

This is to be said three times. When you have done so, breathe three times upon the surface of the mirror, and say:

Come, Anael, come: and let it be thy agreement to be with me willingly: in the name + of the Father, the Most Puissant, in the name + of the Son, Most Wise, in the name + of the Holy Spirit, the Most Living!

Come, Anael, in the terrific name of Jehova! Come, Anael, by the power of the everliving Elohim! Come, thee, by the right arm of the mighty Metatron!

Come to me, N., and order thy subjects so that they may make known to me through their love, joy and peace, the things that are hidden from my eyes.

When you have finished this, raise your eyes toward Heaven and say:

O most powerful Lord, who does cause all things to move in accordance with Thy will, listen to my prayer, and may my intentions be aggreeable to Thee! O Lord, if it be Thy will, deign to gaze upon this mirror and sanctify it, that Thy Servant Anael may come thereto with his companions, and be agreeable to me, N., Thy poor and humble servant! O God, blessed and raised above all the spirits of Heaven, Thou who livest and reignest for all time. Amen.

When this is done, make the Sign of the Cross over yourself, and also on the mirror on the first day, and also on the next fourty and five days. At the end of this time, the angel Anael will appear to you, like unto a beautiful child. He will greet you, and will order his companions to obey you.

It does not always require as loong as this to cause the angel to appear, however. He may come on the fourteenth day, but this will depend upon the degree of application and fervor of the operator.

When he comes, ask him whatever you may desire, and also beg him to come and do your will whenever you shall call him.

When you want Anael to come again, after the first time, all you have to do is to perfume the mirror, and say these words: Come, Anael, come, and let it be thy agreement --and the rest of this prayer to Anael as we have given you above, until the Amen.

DISMISSING THE SPIRIT

When he has answered your questions, and you are satisfied with him, you must send him away by saying this:

I thank thee, Anael, for having appeared and having fulfilled my requests. Thou mayest therefore depart in peace, and shall return when I call unto thee.

The perfume of Anael is saffron.

DIVINATION BY THE WORD OF URIEL

To succeed in this operation, he who makes the experiment must do all things which are told herein. He is to choose a small room or place which for nine days or more has not been visited by women in an impure state [i.e., during their menstration period].

This place must be well cleaned and consecrated, by means of consecrations and aspersions. In the middle of the room there is to be a table covered with a white cloth. On this is a new glass vial full of spring water, brought shortly before the operation, with three small tapers of virgin wax mixed with human fat; a piece of virgin parchment, and the quill of a raven suitable for writing with; an inkpot of chine full of fresh ink; a small container of metal with materials to make a fire.

You must also find a boy of nine or ten years old, who shall be well behaved and cleanly dressed. He should be near the table.

A large new needle is taken, and one of the three tapers is mounted upon it, six inches behind the glass. The other two tapers should be positioned at the right and left of the glass, and an equal distance away.

While you are doing this, say:

Gabamiah, Adonay, Agla, O Lord of Powers, aid us!

Place the virgin parchment on the right of the glass and the pen and ink on the left. Before starting, close the door and windows.

Now stir the fire, and light the wax tapers. Let the boy be on his knees, looking into the glass vial. He should be bareheaded and his hands joined.

Now the Master orders the boy to stare fixedly into the vial, and speaking softly into his right ear, he says:

THE CONJURATION

URIEL + SERAPH + JOSATA + ABLATI + AGLA + CAILA, I beg and conjure thee by the four words that God spoke with His mouth to His servant Moses: JOSTA + AGLA + CAILA + ABLATI. And by the name of the Nine Heavens in which thou livest, and also by the virginity of this child who is before thee, to appear at once, and visibly, to reveal that truth which I desire to know. And when this is done, I shall discharge thee in peace and benevolence, in the Name of the Most Holy Adonay.

When this conjuration is finished, ask the child whether he sees anything in the vial. If he answers that he sees an angel or other materialization, the Master of the operation shall say in a friendly tone:

Blessed spirit, welcome. I conjure thee again, in the Name of the Most Holy Adonay, to reveal to me immediately . . . . (Here the operator petitions the spirit for what he will.)

Then say to the spirit:

If, for any reason, thou dost not wish what thou sayest to be heard by others, I conjure thee to write the answer upon this virgin parchment, between this time and the morrow. Otherwise thou mayst reveal it to me in my sleep.

If the spirit answers audibly, you must listen with respect. If he does not speak, after you have repeated the supplication three times, snuff the tapers, and leave the room until the following day. Return the next morning, and you will find the answer written on the virgin parchment, if it has not been revealed to you in the night.

DIVINATION BY THE EGG

The operation of the Egg is to know what will happen to anyone who is present at the experiment.

One takes an egg of a black hen, laid in the daytime, breaks it, and removes the germ.

You must have a large glass, very thin and clear. Fill this with clear water and into it put the egg-germ.

The glass is placed in the Sun at midday in summer, and the Director of the operation will recite the prayers and conjurations of the day.

These prayers and conjurations are such as are found in the Key of Solomon, in which we treat amply of airy spirits.

And with the index finger, agitate the water, to make the germ turn. Leave it to rest a moment, and then look at it through the glass, not touching it. Then you will see the answer, and it should be tried on a working-day, because these are spirits that will come during the times of ordinary occupations.

If one wishes to see if a boy or a girl is a virgin, the germ will fall to the bottom; and if he (or she) is not, it will be as usual.

TO SEE SPIRITS OF THE AIR

Take the brain of a cock, the powder from the grave of a dead man (which touches the coffin), walnut oil and virgin wax. Make all [this] into a mixture, wrapped in virgin parchment, on which is written the words:

GOMERT KAILOETH, with the character of Khil.

Burn it all, and you will see prodigious things. But this experiment should be done only by those who fear nothing.

To make 3 Girls or 3 Gentlemen appear in your Room, after Supper.

It is necessary to be three days chaste, and you will be elevated.

I. Preparation. On the fourth day, as soon as it is morning, clean and prepare your room, as soon as you have dressed. You must be fasting at this time. Make sure that your room will not be disturbed for the whole of the ensuing day. Note that there shall be nothing hanging, neither anything crosswise to anything else, no tapestries or clothes hanging, and no hats or cages of birds, or curtains of the bed, and so on.

Above all, make sure that everything is clean in every way.

II. Ceremony. After you have supped, go secretly to your room, which has been cleansed as already described. Upon the table there is now to be set a white cloth, and three chairs at the table. In front of each place, set a wheaten roll and a glass of clear and fresh water. Now place a chair at the side of the bed, and retire, while saying this:

III. Conjuration. Besticitum consolatio veni ad me vertat Creon, Creon, Creon, cantor laudem omnipotentis et non commentur. Stat superior carta bient laudem omviestra principiem da montem et inimicos meos o prostantis vobis et mihi dantes que passium fieri sincisibus.

The three people, having arrived, will sit by the fire, eating and drinking, and will thank the person who has entertained them. If you are a gentleman, three girls will come; but if you are a lady, three yound men will be involved.

Then the three will draw lots as to whom is to stay with you. If the operator is a man, the girl who wins will sit in the chair which you have placed by the bed, and she will stay and be with you until midnight. At this time she will leave, with her companions, without having been dismissed.

The two others will stay by the fire, while the first entertains you.

While she is with you, you may ask her any question, about any art or science, or upon any subject at all, and she will at once give you a definite reply. You can ask the whereabouts of hidden treasure, and she will tell you where it is, and how and when to remove it. If the treasure is under the guardianship of infernal spirits, she will come herself, with her companions, and defend you against these fiends.

When she leaves, she will give you a ring. If you wear this on your finger, you will be fortunate at gambling. If you place it on the finger of any woman or girl, you will be able at once to obtain your will of her. Note: The window is to be left open. You can do this experiment as often as you please.

To Make a Girl come to You, however Modest she may Be.

Experiment of a marvelous power of the superior intelligences.

Watch for the crescent or the waning moon, and when you see it, make sure that you see also a star, between the hours of eleven and midnight. Before beginning the process, do thus:

Take a virgin parchment, and write on it the name of the girl whom you desire to come. The shape of the parchment is to be as you see in this figure:

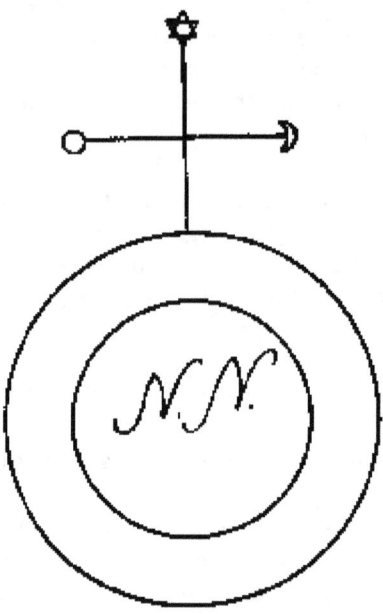

On the other side of the parchment, write MELCHIAEL, BARESCHAS. Then put the parchment on the earth, with the part where the name of the person is written next to the ground. Place your right foot upon the parchment, and your left knee, bent, upon the ground.

Then look to the highest star in the sky, while in this position. In your right hand hold a taper of white wax, sufficiently large to burn for one hour. Then say the following:

THE CONJURATION

I salute thee and conjure thee, O beautiful Moon, O most beautiful Star, O brilliant light which I have in my hand. By the light which I have in my hand. By the air that I breathe within me, by the earth that I am touching: I conjure thee. By the names of the spirit princes living in you. By the ineffable name ON, which created everything! By you, O resplendent angel GABRIEL, with the planet Mercury, Prince, MICHIAEL and MELCHIDÆL.

I conjure you again, by all the Holy Names of God, so that you may send down power to oppress, torture and harass the body and soul and the five senses of N., she whose name is written here, so that she may come unto me. Let her then be tortured, made to suffer. Go, then, at once! Go, MELCHIDÆL, BARESCHES, ZAZEL, FIRIEL, MALCHA, and alll those who are with thee! I conjure you by the Great Living God to obey my will, and I, N., promise to satisfy you.

When this conjuration has been said three times, burn the parchment with the taper. On the next day, take the parchment, put it in your left shoe, and let it stay there until the person whom you have called comes to seek you out. In the conjuration you must say the date that she is to come, and she will not be absent.

TO MAKE ONESELF INVISIBLE

Collect seven black beans. Start the rite on a Wednesday, before sunrise. Then take the head of a dead man, and put one of the black beans in his mouth, two in his eyes and two in his ears. Then make upon his head the character of Morail.

When you have done this, bury the head, with the face upwards, and for nine days, before sunrise, water it each morning with excellent brandy. On the eighth day you will find the spirit mentioned, who will say to you: "What wilt thou?"

You will reply: "I am watering my plant." Then the spirit will say: "Give me the bottle, I desire to water it myself." In answer, refuse him this, even though he will ask you again.

Then he will reach out with his hand, and will display to you that same figure which you have drawn upon the head. Now you can be sure that it is the right spirit, the spirit of the head. There is a danger that another one might try to trick you, which would have evil consequences and in that case your operation would not succeed.

Then you may give him the bottle, and he will water the head and leave. On the next day--which is the ninth--when you return, you will find the beans that are germinating. Take them and put them in your mouth, and look at yourself in the mirror. If you can see nothing, it is well. Test the others in the same way, either in your own mouth, or in that of a child. Those which do not confer invisiblity are to be reburied with the head.

To Have Gold and Silver, or the Hand of Glory

Tear out the hair of a mare in heat, by the roots, closest to the nature, saying DRAGNE, DRAGNE, DRAGNE. Then tie them into a knot. Now go out and buy, without dispute over the price, a new pot of earthenware, which shall have a lid. Return to your house as fast as you can, fill the pot with water from a spring, until it is not quite full. Place the knotted hairs in it, cover it, and place it where neither you nor anyone else can see it, for there is danger in this.

After nine days, at the hidden hour, bring out the pot and open it, and you will find that there is a small animal like a snake therein. This fill jump up. Then say: I ACCEPT THE PACT.

Do not touch the animal with your hand. Place it in a new box, which you have bought for this purpose, and that withouth bargaining as to price. You must feed the creatue on wheat-husks alone, daily.

When you need gold or silver, place as much as you require in the box. Go to bed, with the box at the side of the bed. Sleep, if you desire, for three or four hours. Rise, then, and you will find that the money you have placed in the box has been doubled. But what you put first into the box must be left in it.

If it is an ordinary-looking snake, you should not ask for more than one hundred francs at each time. If, however, it has a human face, then you will be able to obtain a thousand francs each time.

If you want to kill the creature, place in the box instead of its daily husks, some of the flour which has been used fo the consecration in the first Mass said by the priest.After eating this it will die. Above all, do not omit anything, because this is not intended as a joke!

GARTERS FOR DISTANCES

Go out of the house, fasting; march to your left until you find a ribbon-seller. Buy one ell of white ribbon. Pay what is asked, and drop a farthing (un liard) into the box.

Return home by the same route. Next day do the same, until you have found a seller of pens. Buy one, as you bought the ribbon. When you are locked in your own room, write with your own blood on the ribbon the characters of the third line on the plan. This is the right garter. These of the fourth line are for the left. [Shah: These are presumably the planetary symbols in the concentric circles of the plan of the Grimoire.]

When this is done, go out. The third day after, take your ribbon and pen, walk to the left until you find a pastry cook or bakery. Buy a cake or bread for a halfpenny. Go to the first tavern, order a half bottle of wine, have your glass rinsed three times by the same person, break in three the cake or bread.

Put the three pieces in the glass with wine. Take the first piece and throw it under the table without looking at it, saying IRLY, FOR THEE.

Then take the second piece and throw it likewise, saying TERLY, FOR THEE. Write on the other side of the garter the two names of these spirits with your blood. Throw down the third piece, saying, ERLY, FOR THEE. Throw down the pen, drink the wine without eating, pay the cost and go away.

Being outside the town, take the garters, make no mistake as to which is the right and which the left. This is important. Stamp three times with the foot on the ground, pronounce the names a of the spirits TERLY, ERLY, BALTAZARD, IRLY, MELCHIOR, GASPARD, LET US GO. Then make your trip.

To Make a Girl Dance in the Nude

Write on virgin parchment the Character of FRUTIMIERE with the blood of a bat. Then put it on a blessed stone, over which a Mass has been said. After this when you want to use it, place the character under the sill or threshold of a door which she must pass.

When she comes past, she will come in. She will undress and be completely naked, and will dance increasingly until death, if one does not remove the character; with grimaces and contortions which will cause more pity than desire.

To See in a Vision Anything from the Past or Future

The two N N which you see in the second small circle mark the place where you put your name [see To Make a Girl Come to You . . .]. To know what you will, write the names in the circle on virgin parchment, before sleeping, and put it under your right ear on retiring, saying the following orison:

ORISON

O Glorious Name of Great God the ever-living, to whom all things are present, I am Thy servant N. . . . Father Eternal, I beg You to send me Thy Holy Angels, who are written in the Circle and that they shall show me what I want to know, by Jesus Christ our Lord. So be it

Having completed the orison, lie down on your right side, and you will see in a dream that which you desire to know.

To Nail (an Enemy)

Go to a cemetery, remove nailed from an old coffin, saying:

Nails, I take you, so that you may serve to turn aside and cause evil to all persons whom I will. In the Name of the Father, and of the Son, and of the Holy Spirit. Amen..

When you wish to use it, you must look for a footprint and making the three figures of GULAND, SURGAT and MORAIL, fix the nail in the middle saying:

Pater noster upto in terra [our father who art on earth]

Hit the nail with a stone, saying:

Curse evil to N . . ., until I remove thee.

Re-cover the place with a little dust, and remember it well, because one cannot remove the evil which this causes, but by removing the nail, and saying:

I remove thee, so that the evil which thou has caused to N. . ., shall cease. In the Name of the Father, and of the Son. and the Holy Spirit. Amen.

Then take the nail out, and efface the characters: not with the same hand as you make them, but with the other. Thus it will be without danger.

THE SECRET GRIMOIRE OF TURIEL

THE SECRET GRIMOIRE

OF TURIEL

A SYSTEM OF CEREMONIAL MAGIC
THE GREAT ARCANUM
(The Rites of Ceremonial Magick)

PART THE FIRST

OBSERVATIONS AND METHOD OF INVOKING RELATED WITH GREAT PAINS AND DILIGENT RESEARCH

Retire thyself Seven Days free from all company and fast and pray from sunset to sunrise. Rise every morning at Seven of the clock, and the three days previous to the Work fast upon bread and water and humble thyself before Almighty God.

Watch and pray all night before the Work.

And on the day before draw the lines of the Circle in a fair place and let the diameter of the Circle be 9 feet. Wash thyself the same day quite clean. Make the pentacles forthwith and provide the other things necessary, with Incensing. Then being clothed in pure Vestments and having covered the Altar and lighted the candies begin about half an hour before sunrise on the Day assigned for the Work and say with great Devotion as follows

FIRST MORNING PRAYER

Almighty and Most Merciful Father I beseech Thee that Thou wilt vouchsafe favorably to hear me at this time whilst I make my humble prayer and Supplication unto Thee. I confess unto Thee O Lord Thou hast justly punished me for my manifold sins and offences but Thou hast promised at what time so ever a sinner doth repent of his sins and wickedness Thou wilt pardon and forgive him and turn away the remembrance of them from before Thy face.

Purge me therefore O Lord and wash me from all my offences in the Blood of Jesus Christ that, being pure and clothed in the Vestments of Sanctity, I may bring this Work to perfection, through Jesus our Lord who liveth and reigneth with Thee in the Unity of the Holy Ghost. Amen.

Sprinkle thyself with Holy Water and say

Asperges me Domine hysope, et mundabor. Lavabis me et super nivem dealbabor.

Hail O Mighty God, for in Thy power alone abideth the Key to all exorcising of Principalities, Powers, Thrones, Angels and Spirits. Amen.

Then bless your Girdle, saying

O God Who by the breath of Thy nostrils framed Heaven and Earth and wonderfully disposed all things therein in six days, grant that this now brought to perfection by Thine unworthy servant may be by Thee blessed and receive Divine virtue, power and Influence from Thee that every thing therein contained may fully operate according to the hope and confidence of me Thine time worthy servant through Jesus Christ our Lord and Saviour. Amen.

THE BLESSING OF THE LIGHT

I bless thee in the Name of the Father. O Holy, Holy Lord, God, Heaven and Earth are fuil of Thy Glory before Whose face there is a bright shining light forever; bless now, O Lord, I beseech Thee, these creatures of light which Thou hast given for the Kindly use of man that they, by Thee being sanctified, may not be put out or extinguished by the power, malice, or filthy darkness of the devil, but may shine forth brightly and lend their assistance to this my Work, through Jesus Christ our Lord. Amen.

Then say, 'Asperges me, etc."

CONSECRATION OF THE SWORD

O Great God Who art the God of strength and fortitude and greatly to be feared, bless O Lord, this Instrument that it may be a terror unto the Enemy, and therewith I may fight with and overcome all phantasms and oppositions of the Enemy, through the influence and help of Thy most Holy Mighty Name, On, St. Agla, and in the Cross of Jesus Christ our only Lord. Amen.

Be thou blessed and consecrated in the Name of the Father, Son, and Holy Ghost. Asperges me, etc.

BENEDICTION OF THE LAMENS
(SYMBOIS. CIRCLES)

O God Thou God of my Salvation I call upon Thee by the mysteries of Thy most holy Name, On, St. Agla, I worship and beseech Thee by Thy Names El, Elohim, Elohe, Zebaoth, and by Thy Mighty Name Tetragrammaton, Saday, that Thou wilt be seen in the power and force of these Thy most holy names so written filling them with divine virtue and Influence through Jesus Christ our Lord.

BENEDICTION OF THE PENTACLES

Eternal God which, by Thy Holy Wisdom, hast caused great power and virtue to lie hidden in the characters and Holy Writings of Thy Spirits and Angels, and hast given unto man that with them, faithfully used, power thereby to work many things; bless these, O Lord, framed and written by the hand of me Thine unworthy servant that being filled with divine virtue and Influence by Thy Commands, O Most Holy God, they may shew forth their virtue and power to Thy praise and Glory through Jesus Christ our Lord. Amen.

I bless and consecrate you in the Name of the Father, the Son, and the Holy Ghost, the God of Abraham, Isaac, and Jacob. Asperges me, etc. Amen.

BENEDICTION OF THE GARMENT

O Holy, blessed and Eternal Lord God Who art the God of purity and delightest that our souls should appear before Thee in clean and pure and undefiled Vestments being cleansed, blessed, and consecrated by Thee, I may put them on, being therewith clothed I may be whiter than snow both in soul and body in Thy presence this day, in and through the ment, death, and passion of our onty Lord and Saviour Jesus Christ, Who liveth and reigneth with Thee in the Unity of the Holy Spirit, ever one God, world without end. The God of Abraham, Isaac and Jacob bless thee, purge thee, and make thee pure, and be thou clean in the Name of the Father, Son and Holy Ghost. Amen.

In this Thy Holy Sign O God, I fear no evil. By Thy Holy Power, and by this Thy Holy Sign all evil doth flee.

By Thy Holy Name and Thy Power which Secret was revealed to Moses, through the Holy Names written in this Book, depart far from me all ye workers of iniquity.

Bless, O Lord, I beseech Thee, this place and drive away all evil and wickedness far from it. Sanctify and make it become meet and convenient for Thy Servant to finish and bring to pass therein his desires, through Jesus Christ our Lord, Amen.

Be thou blessed and purified in the Name of the Father, Son, ami Holy Ghost. Amen.

BENEDICTION OF THE PERFUMES

The God of Abraham, the God of Isaac, the God of Jacob, bless here the creatures of these kinds that they may give forth the power of their odours so that neither the Enemy nor any false Imaginaions may be able to enter into them, through our Lord Jesus Christ, to whom be honour and Glory now, henceforth, and for ever. Amen.

Sprinkle them with Holy Water, saying, "Asperges me, Domine, etc."

EXORCISM OF FIRE

I exorcise thee, O thou creature of Fire, by Him by Whom all things are made, that forthwith thou wilt cast away every phantasm from thee that it shall not be able to do any hurt in any thing. Bless, O Lord, this creature of Fire and sanctify it, that it may be biessed to set forth the praise of Thy Holy Name that no hurt may be able to come unto me, through the virtue and defence of our Lord Jesus Christ. Amen.

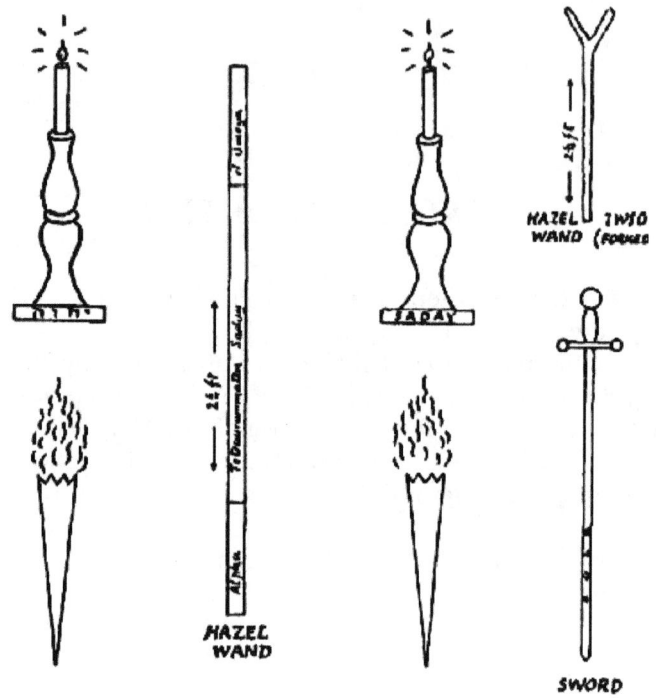

INVOCATION FOR SUNDAY
(SOL)

Come, Heavenly Spirits who have the effulgent rays of the Sun, Luminous Spirits who are ready to obey the power of the great Tetragrammaton, come and assist me in the operation that I am making under the auspices of the Grand Light of Day whicb the Eternal Creator hath formed for the use of universal nature. I invoke you for these purposes. Be favourable and auspicious to what I shall ask in the Name of Amioram, Adonai, Sabaoth.

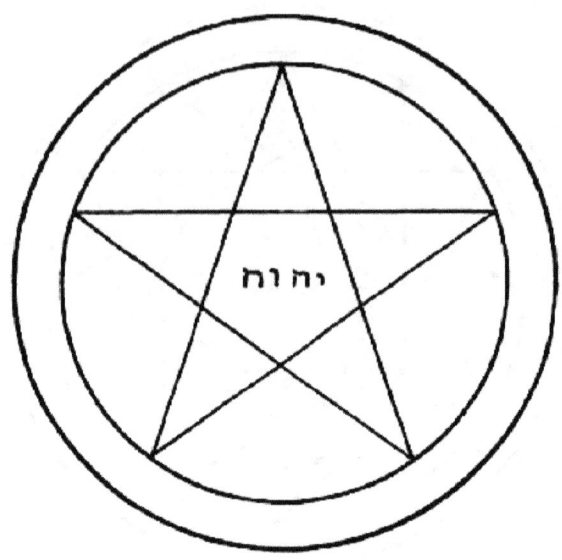

INVOCATION FOR MONDAY
(MOON)

Haste ye Sublime and Intelligent Genil who are obedient to the Sovereigu Arcana, come and assist me in the operation that I undertake under the auspices of the Grand Lumiriary of the Night. I invoke you to this end and implore you to be favourable and hear my entreaties in the Name of Him Who commands the spirits of the Four Quarters of the Universal Mansions: Inhabit, Bileth, Mizabu, Abinzaba.

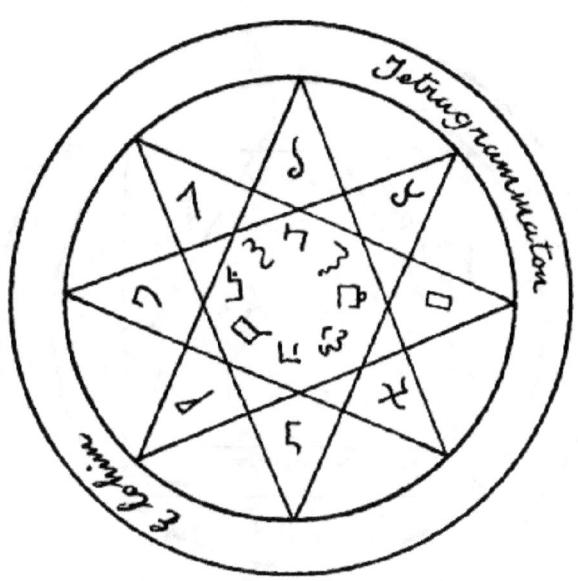

INVOCATION FOR TUESDAY
(MARS)

Come Children of the Red Genii who have executed the order of the Sovereign Master of the Universe upon the armies of the rash Sennacherib, come and assist me in the operation that I undertake under the auspices of the third brilliant luminary of the firmament; be favourable to my entreaties in the Name of Adonay Sabaoth.

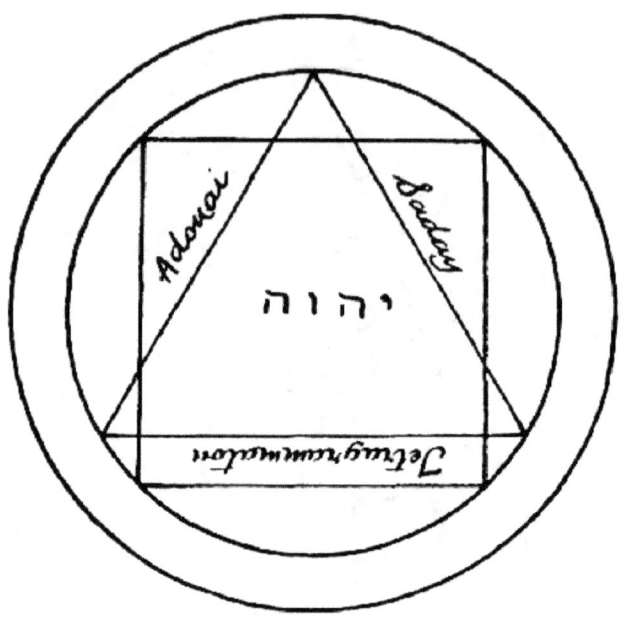

INVOCATION OF WEDNESDAY
(MERCURY)

Run to me with speed, come to me ye Spirits of Mercury who preside over the operation of this day, hear favourably the present invocation that I make to you under the Divine Names of Venoel, Uranel, be kind and ready to second my undertakings. Render them efficacious.

INVOCATION FOR THURSDAY
(JUPITER)

Come speedily ye Olepid Spirits who preside over the operation of this day.

Come, Incomprehensible Zebarel and all your legions, haste to my assistance and be propitious to my undertakings, be kind and refuse me not your powerful aid and assistance.

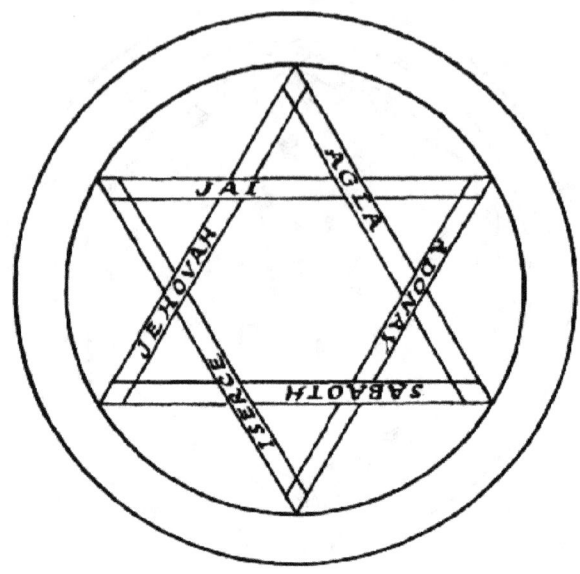

INVOCATION FOR FRIDAY
(VENUS)

Come on the wings of the wind, ye happy Genii who preside over the workings of the heart. Come in the Name of the Great Tetragrammaton; hear favourably the Invocation that I make this day, destined to the wonder of love. Be ready to lend me your assistance to succeed in what I have undertaken under the hope that you will be favourable to me.

INVOCATION FOR SATURDAY
(SATURN)

Come out of your gloomy solitude ye Saturnine spirits, come with your cohort, come with diligence to the place where I am going to begin my operation under your auspices; be attentive to my labours and contribute your assistance that it may rebound to the honour and glory of the Highest.

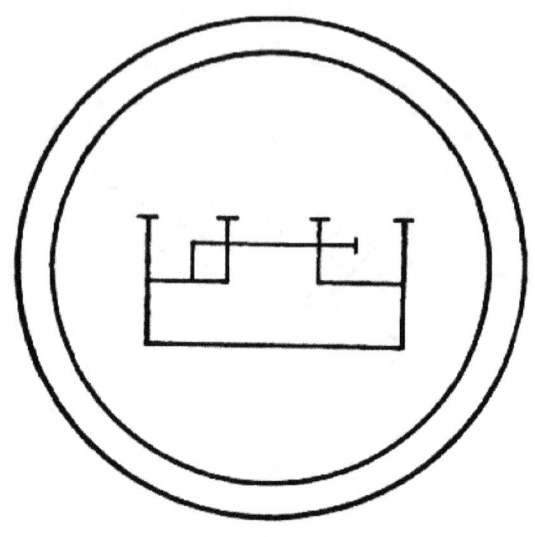

CHARACTER OF ARATRON
LORD OF SATURN

PERFUMES

Saifron, with the wood of Aloes, the Elder and the Pine. Add to it a grain of Musk, and consecrate the whole, pulverized and mixed together in a paste.

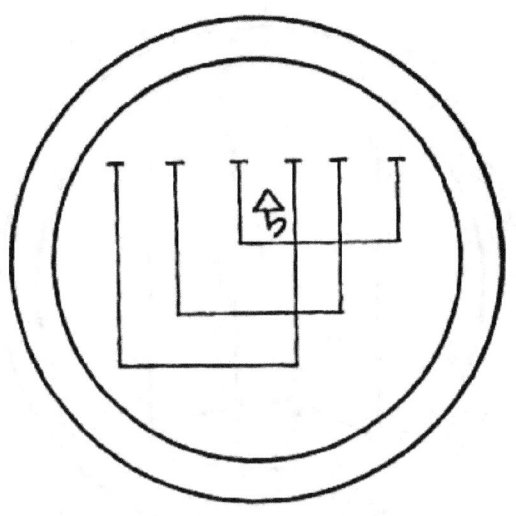

CHARACTER OF PRALEG
LORD OF MARS

PERFUMES

The head of a frog, the Bovine Blood, a grain of White Poppy, Flowers of Camomile, and Camphor, pulverized into a paste by the mixing of the blood of a Virgin Kid.

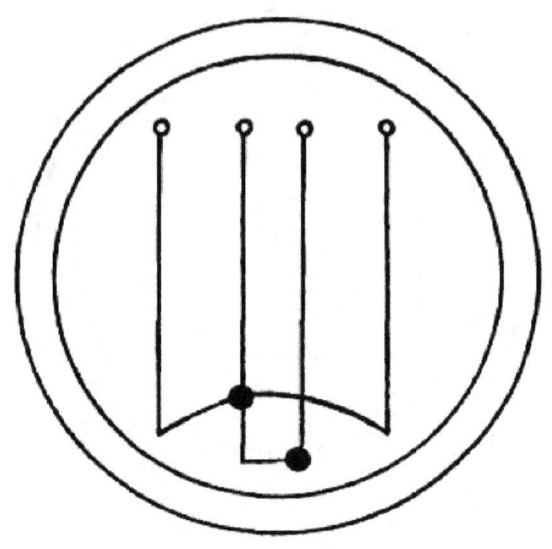

CHARACTER OF PHUL
LORD OF THE MOON

PERFUMES

Leaves of the Mandrake, Sal Ammonia, Roots of Gentian, Valerian herbs finely cut, a little Sulphur, made into a paste with the blood of a black Cat.

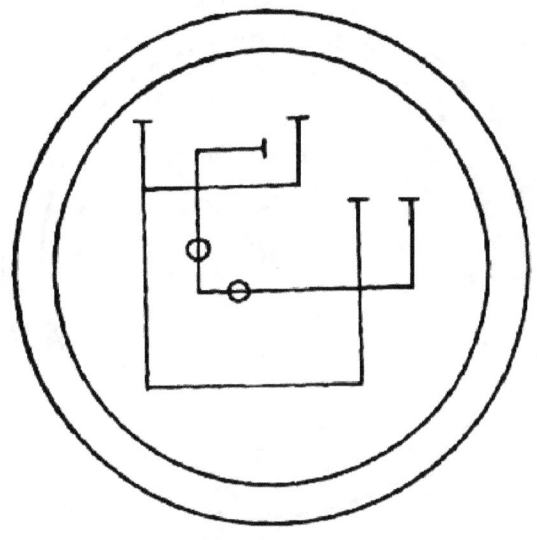

CHARACTER OF JETHOR
LORD OF JUPITER

PERFUMES

Sandalwood of the East, leaves of Agrimony, Choves, powder of Henbane. Beat all into a powder. Make thereof a paste with Foxes' blood and the brains of a Magpie.

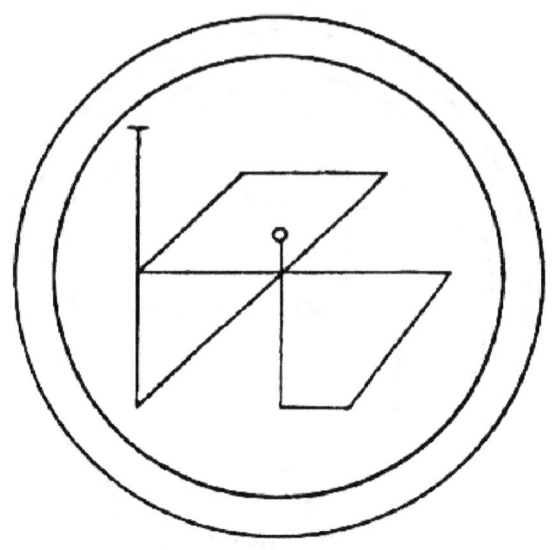

CHARACTER OF OPHIEL
LORD OF MERCURY

PERFUMES

The seed of an Ash Tree, the wood of the Aloe, leaves of the Scullcap Herb, Mandrake roots, and the end of a Quill, made into small balls (pihis).

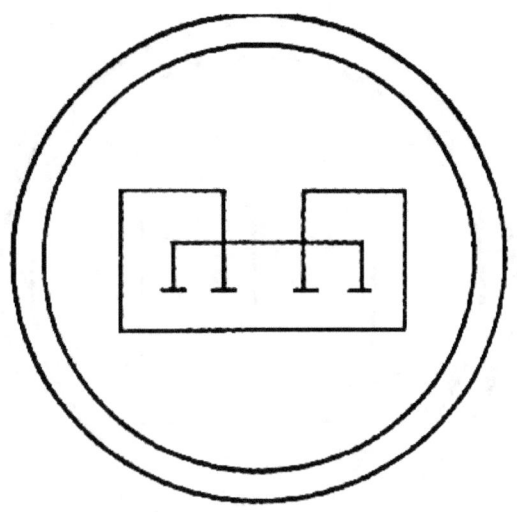

CHARACTER OF HAGITH
LORD OF VENUS

PERFUMES

Musk, Juniper berries, wood of Aloes, dried Red Roses, dried leaves of Elder, pulverized, and made into a paste with the blood of a Pigeon.

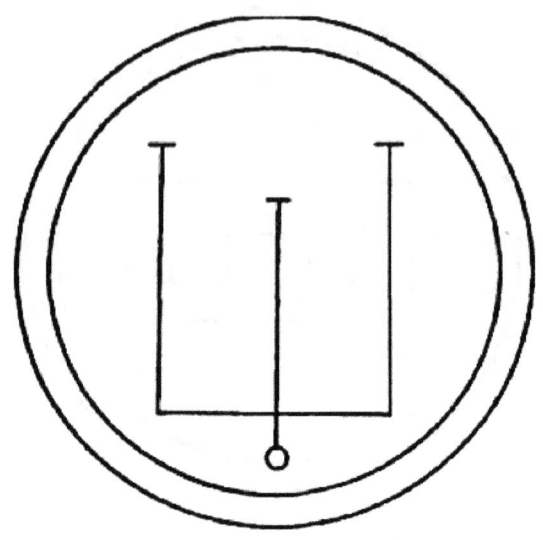

CHARACTER OF OCH
LORD OF THE SUN

PERFUMES

Grains of Bhack Pepper, grains of Hogsbane, powder of Sulphur, made into a paste with the blood of a Bat, and the brains of a black Cat.

PART THE SECOND

CONTAINING INVOCATIONS, CONJURATIONS, ARO EXORCISMS OF TREE BAND OF SPIRITS

FORM OF CONJURING AND EXORCISING SPIRITS

Oration to be said when putting on the Vestures

Amacor, Amacor, Amides, Theodomai, Aintor, by the merits of Thy Angels, O Lord, I with I put on the garments of Righteousness, that this which I desire I may bring to perfection through the most holy Adonay, Whose kingdom endureth for ever and ever. Amen.

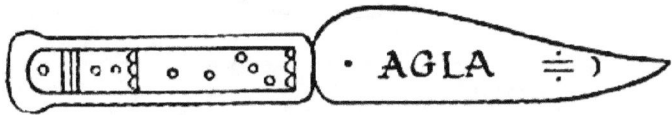

This on the other side

The Lamen

PRAYER

Holy, Holy Lord God, from Whom all holy desires do proceed, I beg Thou wilt be merciful unto me at this time, granting I may become a True Magician and contemplate of Thy wondrous works at alt times, in the Name of the Father and of the Son. Therefore in al! my doings and at all times I will call upon Thy Most Holy Name, O Lord, for Thy help and assistance.

I beseech Thee, O Lord, that Thou wilt purge me and wash me iii the blood of our Saviour, from al! my sins and frailties, and that Thou wilt henceforward vouchsafe to keep and defend me from pride, lusts, cursing, blasphemy, unfaithfulness, and al! other deadly sins and enormous offences, profaneness and spiritual wickedness ; but that I may lead a godhy, saber, faithful, constant and pure life, walking uprightly in Thy sight, through the merits of Jesus Christ, Thy Son, our Lord and Saviour.

Omnipotent and Eternal Lord God Who sittest in Heaven and dost from thence behoid alt the dwehlers upon earth, most mercifully I beseech Thee to hear and answer the petition of Thine unworthy servant, which I shali make unto Thee at this time, through Jesus Christ our Lord, Who hiveth and reigneth with Thee in the unity of Thy Holy Spirit, ever One God, world without end.

Sead down, O Lord, the Spirit of Thy Grace upon me. O God, put fear far from me, and give me an abundance in Thy faith, whereby all things are made possible unto man; put every wicked phantom far from my mind, and grant me true zeal, fervor, and intentive spirit of zeal, and prayer, that I may offer up a well-pleasing sacrifice unto Thee. Let me use Thy ministering spirits and

Angels, O Lord, as thereby I may attain true wisdom and knowledge.

Our Father, etc.

Credo, etc.

Ave Maria, etc.

Glory be to the Father, Son, and Holy Ghost; as it was in the beginning, is now, and ever shalll be, world without end. Amen.

Holy, Holy, Holy, Lord God of Sabaoth, which will come to judge the quick and the dead; Thou art Alpha and Omega, the first and the last, King of Kings, and Lord of Lords, Ioth, Abiel, Anathiel, Aniasim, Alganabro, El, Sedomel, Gayes, Hehi, Messias, Tolosm, Elias, Eschiros, Athanatos; by these Thy Holy Names, and al! others, I do call upon Thee and beseech Thee, O Lord, by Thy Nativity and baptism, by Thy Cross and Passion, by Thine ascension, and by the coming of Thy Holy Ghost, by the bitterness of Thy Soul when it departed from Thy body; by Thine Angels, Archangels, prophets, patriarchs, and by all Thy Saints, and by alt the Sacraments which are made in Thine honour, I do worship and beseech Thee, I bless and desire Thee, to accept these prayers and conjurations. I implore Thee, O Holy Adonay, Amay, Horta, Vegadoro, Ysion, Ysesy, and by all Thy Holy Names, and by al! Thine Angels, Archangels, and Powers, Dominations, and Virtues, and by Thy Name with which King Solomon did bind up the devils and shut them up, Ethrack, Evanher, Agla, Goth, Joth, Othie, Venock, Nabrat, and by all Thy Holy Names which are written in this book, and by the virtue of them all, that Thou enable me to congregate all Thy spirits, that they may give me true answers to all my demands.

O Great and Eternal Virtue of the Highest, which Thou disposest their being come to judgment, Viachem, Stimilomaton, Esphares, Tetragrammaton, Oboram, Cryon, Elijtion, Onela, Brassim, Aoym, Messias, Soter, Emanuel, Sabaoth, Adonay, I worship Thee. I implore Thee with all the strength of my mind that by Thee my present prayers, consecrations, and conjurations may be hallowed. In the Name of the most merciful God of Heaven and of Earth, of the Seas and of the Infernais, by Thine Omnipotent help may I perform this Work.

Helie, Helion, Esseju, Deus Eternis, Eloy, Clemens Deus, Sanctus Sabaoth, Deus Exercillum, Adonay, Deus Mirabilis, Jao, Verax, Ampheneton, Saday, Dominator, On, Fortissimus Deus, invest with Thy blessed help this Work begun of Thee, that it may be consummated by Thy mighty power. Amen.

Amoruli, Tametia, Latisten, Rabur, Tanetia, Latisten, Escha, Aloelin, Alpha et Omega, Leytse, Oraston, Adonay. Amen.

NAMES AND OFFICES OF THE SPIRITS MESSENGERS AND INTELLIGENCES OF THE SEVEN PLANETS

SPIRITS OF THE SUN
Gabriel
Vianathraba
Corat

MESSENGERS OF THE SUN
Burchat
Suceratos
Capabile

INTELLIGENCES OF THE SUN
Haludiel
Machasiel
Chassiel

SPIRITS OF THE MOON
Gabriel
Gabraei
Madios

MESSENGERS OF THE MOON
Anael
Pabael
Ustael

INTELLIGENCES OF THE MOON
Uriel
Naromiel
Abuori

SPIRITS OF SATURN
Samael
Bachiel
Astel

MESSENGERS OF SATURN
Sachieh
Zoniel
Hubaril

INTELLIGENCES OF SATURN
Mael
Orael
Valnum

SPIRITS OF JUPITER
Setchiel
Chedusitanieh
Corael

MESSENGERS OF JUPITER
Tunel
Conieh
Babiel

INTELLIGENCES OF JUPITER
Kadiel
Maltiel
Huphatrieb
Estael

SPIRITS OF VENUS
Thamael
Tenariel
Arragon

MESSENGERS OF VENUS
Coiznas
Peajel
Penael

INTELLIGENCES OF VENUS
Penat
Thiel
Rael
Teriapel

SPIRITS OF MERCURY
Mathlai
Tarmiel
Baraborat

MESSENGERS OF MERCURY
Raphael
Ramel
Doremiel

INTELLIGENCES OF MERCURY
Aiediat
Modiat
Sugmonos
Sallales

PRESIDING SPIRITS OF JUPITER.
Sachiel
Castiel
Asasiel

PRESIDING SPIRITS OF VENUS
Anael
Rachiel
Sachiel

PRESIDING SPIRITS OF MARS
Samael
Satael
Amabiel

PRESIDING SPIRITS OF MERCURY
Raphael

Uriel
Seraphiel

Angeli Glorioso supradicti estote coadjutores et auxiliatores in omnibus negotijs et interrogationibus in omnibus celensq causis per Eum qui venturus est judiciase vivos et mortuos.

Omnipotent and Eternal God Who hast ordained the whole creation for Thy praise and glory and for the salvation of man, I earnestly beseech Thee that Thou wouldst send one of Thy spirits of the Orden of Jupiter, one of the messengers of Sachiel whom Thou hast appointed presiding spirit of Thy firmament at this time, most faithfully, willingly to show unto me those things which I shall demand or require of him, and truly execute my desires. Nevertheless, O most Holy God, Thy will and not mine be done, through Jesus Christ our Lord. Amen.

INVOCATION

I call upon thee, Sachiel, Castiel, and Asasiel, in the Name of the Father, and of the Son, and of the Holy Ghost, Blessed Trinity, Inseparable Unity, I invoke and entreat thee, Sachiel, Castiel, and Asasiel, in this hour to attend to the words and conjurations which I shall use by the Holy Names of God, El, Elohim, Elohe, Eeoba, Sabaoth, Elion, Eschiros, Adonay, Jay, Tetragrammaton, Saday; I conjure and excite you by the Holy Names of God, Hagios, Otheos, Ischyros, Athanatos, Paracletos, Agla, On, Alpha and Omega, Ausias, Tolimi, Elias, Irnos, Aniay, Horta, Vegadora, Antir, Sibranat, Amatha, Baldachia, Anuoram, Anexpheton, Via,Vita, Manus, Fons, Origo,Filius

and by all the other Holy, Glorious, Great, and Unspeakable, Mysterious, Mighty, Powerful, and Incomprehensible Names of God, that you attend unto the words which I shall utter, and send unto me Tarje!, Coniel, on Babiel, messengers of your sphere, to tell unto me such things as I shall demand of him, in the Name of the Father, Son, and Holy Ghost.

I entreat thee, Setchiel, Chedustaniel, and Corael, by the whole host of Heaven, Seraphims, Cherubims, Thrones, Dominations, Virtues, Powers, Principalities, Archangels and Angels, by the great and giorious Spirits Orphaniel, Tetra, Pagiel, Salmia, Pastor, Salun, Azimor, and by your Star which is Jupiter, and by all the constellations of Heaven, and by whatsoever you obey, and by your Character which you have given and proposed and confirmed, that you attend unto me according to the prayers and petitions which I have made unto Almighty God, and that you forthwith send unto me one of your messengers who may willingly and truly and faithfully fulfill all my desires, wishes and commands, and that you command him to appear unto me in form of a beautiful angel clothed in white vestures, gently, courteously, kindly, and affably entering into communication with me, and that he neither bring terror nor fear unto me, or obstinately deny my requests, neither permitting any evil spirits to appear or approach in any way to hurt, terrify, or affright me, nor deceiving me in any wise; through the virtue of our Lord and Saviour Jesus Christ, in Whose Name I attend, waiting for and expecting your appearance. Fiat, Fiat, Fiat. Amen.

INTERROGATIONS

"Comest thou in peace, in the Name of the Father, and of the Son, and of the Holy Ghost "

"Yes".

"Thou art welcome, noble Spirit. What is thy name?"

"Turiel ".

"I have called thee here, Turiel, in the Name of Jesus of Nazareth, at Whose Name every knee doth bow, both of things in Heaven, Earth, and Heil, and every tongue shall confess there is no Name like unto the Name of Jesus, Who hath given power unto man to bind and to loose all things in His Name, yea, even unto them that trust in His salvation. Art thou the messeager of Setchiel"

"yes"

"Wilt thou confirm thyself unto me at this time, and from henceforward reveal all things unto me that I shall desire to know and teach me how to increase my wisdom and knowledge, and show unto me the secrets of the Magick Art, and of the liberal sciences, that I may set forth the praise and glory of Almighty God"
"Yes".

"Then, I pray thee, give and confirm thy Character unto me, whereby I may call thee at al! times, and also swear unto me this Oath, and I will righteously keep my vow and covenant unto Almighty God, and will courteously receive thee at all times when thou dost appear to me

"Forasmuch as thou camest in peace and quietness and hast answered me and unto my petitions, I give humble and hearty thanks unto Almighty God, in whose Name I called thee and thou camest. And now thou mayest depart in peace unto thy Orders, and return unto me again at what time soever I shall call thee by Licence to Depart

"thine own Oath, or by thy name, or by thine Order, or by thine Office which is granted from the Creator. And the Grace of God be with thee and me and upon the whoie Israel of God. Amen.

"Glory be to the Father, and to the Son, and to the Holy Ghost, as it was in the beginning, is now, and ever shall be, world without end. Fiat. Fiat. Fiat. Amen ".

Form of a Bond of Spirits given by Turiel, Messenger of the Spirits of Jupiter:

Gloria Deo in Excelsis.

I, Turiel, Messenger of the Spirits of Jupiter, appointed thereunto by the Creator of all things visible and invisible, do swear and promise, and plighting faith and troth unto thee in the presence, by, and before the Great Lord of Heaven and the whole company of Heaven, by all the Holy Names of God, do swear and bind myself unto thee, by all the contents of God's Sacred Writ, by the Incarnation, death and passion, resurrection, and glorious Ascension of Jesus Christ, by all the Holy Sacraments, by the Mercy of God, by the Glory and Eyes of Heaven, by the forgiveness of sin, and hope of eternal salvation, by the Great

Day of Doom, by all the Angels and Archangels, Seraphim, Cherubim, Dominations, Thrones, Principalities, Powers, and Virtues, Patriarchs, Prophets, Saints, Martyrs, Innocents, and all others of the blessed and glorious Company of Heaven, and by all the sacred powers and virtues above rehearsed, and by whatever is holy and binding, thus do I swear now, and promise unto thee that I will hasten unto thee, and appear clearly unto thee at all times and places, and in all hours, days, and minutes, from this time forward until thy life's end, whensoever thou shalt call me by my name, or by my Office, and will come unto thee in what form thou shalt desire, whether it be visibly or invisibly; I will answer all thy desires. And in testimony whereof, and before all the Powers of Heaven, I have hereunto set, subscribed, and confirmed my Character unto thee.

So help me God. Fiat. Amen.

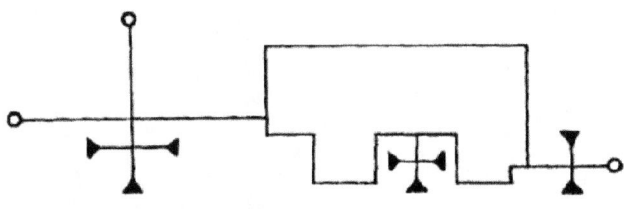

THE CHARACTER OF TURIEL

FINIS

THE BLACK PULLET

THE BLACK PULLET

OR

THE HEN WITH THE GOLDEN EGGS

"Comprising the Science of Magical Talismans and Rings; the art of Necromancy and the Kabbalah, for conjuring the aerial and infernal spirits, sylphs, undines, and gnomes; for acquiring knowledge of the secret sciences; for discovering treasures, for the gaining of power to command all beings, and for unmasking all evil spells and sorceries," From the teachings of Socrates, Pythagoras, Plato, Zoroaster, son of the great Aromasis, and other philosophers whose manuscripts escaped the burning of Ptolemy's library, and translated from the language of the Magi and of the Hieroglyphs, by the Doctors Mizzaboula-Jabamia, Danhuzerus, Nehmahmian, Judahim, Eliaeb, and translated into French by A.J.S .D.R.L.G.F. in Egypt 740.

PREFACE

The work which we offer to the public must not be confused with a collection of reveries and errors to which their authors have tried to give credence by announcing supernatural feats; which the credulous and the ignorant seized with avidity. We only quote the most respectable authorities and most dignified in faith. The principles which we present are based on the doctrines of the ancients and modern, who full of respect for the Divinity, were always the friends of mankind, endeavoured to recall them to virtue, by showing them vice in all its deformity. We have drawn from the most pure sources, having only in view the love of truth and the desire to enlighten those who desire to discover the secrets of Nature and the marvels which they unfold to those who never separate the darkness which surrounds them. It is only given to those who are favoured by The Great Being, to raise themselves above the terrestrial sphere, and to plan a bold flight in the etheric regions; it is for these privileged men that we write.

To us no importance is given to the splenetic Voices which are raised against us. The silence and the smile of disdain will be the only answer with which We shall oppose them, and we shall follow with firm Sustained steps the route which indicates to us the luminous stars which fill the heavens, which cover our heads, and which light these thousands of worlds, which bless every day with our Sovereign Master of the Universe, which He has created, also ourselves, and whose Will maintains this admirable order, Which commands our admiration, our respect and our love.

THE BLACK PULLET

Before beginning the subject, and to acquaint my readers of this profound Science, which until the present day has been the object of research of the most constant and profound meditations, I must unbosom myself how these marvelous secrets were communicated to me, and the manner in which the Divine Providence allowed me to escape from the greatest dangers and, so to speak, conducted me by the Divine Hand, to prove that by Divine Will it is sufficient to raise unto Himself the last of Beings or to precipate to naught those who are clothed with all power on Earth. We all therefor come from God, God is everything, and without God nothing can exist. Who more than I may penetrate the truth eternal and sacred.
I formed part of the expedition to Egypt, an officer in the army of the genius. I took part in the successes and reverses of this army, which victorious or obliged to cede to force from the eventualities and circumstances, always covered itself with glory.

As there is no point in relating here any detail which deals with this memorable campaign, I will but relate one single feature, with which I was touched, and is necessary for the development which I must give to those whom I mentioned in my preface. I had been sent by the General, under whose orders I found myself, to draw up the plans of the Pyramids; he had given me an escort of some mounted light infantry horse. I arrived with them at my destination without experiencing any accident, also without noticing anything that could conjecture the fate that awaited us.

We had dismounted near the Pyramids, our horses had been tethered; sitting on the sands we appeased the hunger that tormented us. French gaiety seasoned the food which composed our frugal meal. It was on the point of ending, and I was occupied with my work when all of a sudden a horde of desert Arabs fell on us. We did not have the time to place ourselves in a position of defence. The blows of swords descended upon us, the bullets whistled, and I received several wounds. My unhappy companions were lying on the ground dead or expiring. Our cruel enemies after having removed our weapons and clothes, disappeared with our horses with the speed of lightning. I remained for some time in a state of prostration, facing the sun. At last recovering some of my strength, I raised myself with pain. I had two sword cuts on the head, and one on the left arm. I looked around me. I saw nothing but corpses, a burning sky and arid sand in an immense desert and a frightning solitude. With but the hope of a certain and cruel death, I resigned myself to saying goodbye to my country to my parents and to my friends. Invoking heaven, I crawled to the Pyramid, and the blood which ran with abundance from my wounds reddened the sand which was soon to be my tomb.

Arriving at the foot of these worldly marvels I sat down and leaned against this enormous mass that had seen many centuries pass by and which would see many more pass. I thought that my existence which was soon to end had come to naught just as the day which was nearing its end, the sun being on the point of plunging into the ocean.

"Brilliant star, receive my goodbyes," I said with emotion. "My eyes will never see you again, your benificent light will never shine on me again. Goodbye." As I said this goodbye which I thought was eternal, the sun disappeared. The night came and covered the world with its dark curtain.

I was absorbed with the most sad reflections when a light noise could be heard a few paces from me. A large slab of stone detached itself from the pyramid and fell on the sand; I turned to that side, and by the light of a small lantern that he carried in his hand, I perceived a venerable old man who came out of the pyramid. A white beard covered his chest, a turban covered his head, and the rest of his costume indicated that he was a Mohammedan. He cast his eyes around; then advancing a few steps he halted opposite the corpse of one of my unhappy companions of misfortune.

"Oh Heavens!" he cried in Turkish. "A man is wounded, a Frenchman is dead." He lifted his eyes to the sky saying: "Oh Allah." He then discovered the others which he carefully examined to see if he could not find one who still breathed, and to assure himself, I saw him place his hand in the region of the heart. The old man recognised that they had all ceased to live. Uttering a painful groan, with tears furrowing down from his eyes, he retraced his steps to re-enter the pyramid. I felt the desire to conserve my days. I had already made the sacrifice of my life; hope entered my heart. Summoning all my strength, I called to him; he heard me, and turning his lantern in my direction, he saw me. Advancing he gave me his hand, which I seized and pressed to my ups. He saw that I was wounded and that blood was flowing from the cuts on my head.

Placing his lantern on the ground, he removed his girdle and covered my brow. He then helped me to get up. I had lost a lot of blood and was suffering from extreme weakness—I hardly had the strength to support myself. Placing his lantern in my hand, then taking me in his arms, he carried me near the opening in the pyramid from which he had come and placed me gently on the sand. Giving me an affectionate grip of the hand, he indicated that he was re-entering the pyramid and would return promptly.

I gave thanks to Heaven for the unexpected help that had been sent me. The old man reappeared carrying a flagon. He removed the cork and poured a few drops of the liqueur into a drinking vessel which he gave to me to drink. A delicious perfume diffused around me. Hardly had this Divine Liqueur penetrated my stomach than I felt regenerated, and I had enough strength to enter the pyramid with my benefactor and generous conductor.

We then stopped for a few moments. He replaced the stone that had fallen, which he adjusted with an iron bar, and we descended by an easy slope into the interior of the pyramid. After having walked for some time on the same path, which made several sinuous turns, we arrived at a door which he secretly opened and closed with care. Then having crossed an immense hall, we entered another place. A lamp hung from the ceiling; there was a table covered with books, several oriental divans or seats, and a bed on which to rest. The kind old man conducted me to a seat where he made me sit down. Placing his lantern on the table he opened a kind of cupboard from which he took several vases.

He approached me and invited me to remove my clothes with an attention and complaisance difficult to describe. Having examined my wounds he applied with solemn formality several balms which came from the vases of which I have previously spoken. Hardly had they been applied to my arms and head than the pains were soothed. He invited me to lie on his bed, and very soon a beneficial and soothing sleep weighed down my eyelids.

When I awoke, I looked around and saw sitting near me the good old man who did not wish to partake of rest while I was asleep as he feared that I might need help. I tendered him my most grateful thanks by the most expressive signs. In the same manner he signified to me that I must remain quiet. He gave me a new portion of the cordial which had already proved its happy effects. Afterwards he looked at me with extreme attention, and realizing that he had nothing to fear for my life, he affectionately patted my hand. He then lay down on some cushions on the other side of the chamber where we were, and soon I heard him sleeping profoundly and peacefully.

"Oh benevolent one," I said to myself, "thou art virtue par excellance and a pure emanation of the Divinity; thou unitest and bringest men together and thou makest them forget the pains to which they are prey. Through thee they are returned to happiness, and too thou art this happiness, the object of all their wishes and all their desires."

My host made a movement and got up. He came to me and smiled at seeing me in a state of calm and tranquility which left him in no fear of my being. He gave me to understand that he was going to leave me so that he could go out of the pyramid and see what was happening outside. He brought to my side that which he thought would be necessary for my needs, and then he left me alone.

Until this moment I had not reflected at all on what had happened to me in this exigency. I found myself safe in this subterranean place, and I had no uneasiness relative to my host; however, this would have to come to an end by my departing after I had been cured and re-joining the Army. I was occupied with these ideas when I saw the old man re-enter. He gave me to understand that several Arab corps and Mamelouks were surveying the plain and that he had seen them without being noticed because his retreat was impenetrable to all eyes. He indicated that he had me in his care and regarded me as his son; therefore I could deliver myself to the greatest security. I indicated to him my complete gratitude, and he appeared satisfied. As I appeared to be dissatisfied to be able to express myself only by signs, he brought me a book indicating that with its help we could soon communicate together without hesitation. The career which I had followed since my childhood had familiarised me with meditation, I loved the application of mind, and I was soon in the condition to listen to my generous old man. He also showed such compliance in the lessons which he gave me that even with less good will, one would have made progress. I remain silent on all that was relative to my new education. My complete cure and convalescence took longer than I realized. My host went out from time to time to see what was taking place as he was in complete ignorance of earthly events.

In short, one day he was longer than usual, and on his return he informed me that the French Army had evacuated Egypt and that I could not hope to leave at this time without giving an account of the days that I had spent with him. I should stay with him which he would make me do by his kindness and love so that in my particular case of captivity my fate would not be as cruel as I might think because he would teach me things which would astonish me and I should desire nothing in the way of good fortune. I had begun to understand the Turkish language. He told me to get up. I obeyed him. He took me by the hand and conducted me to the end of the chamber. He opened a door opposite the one by which one entered, and taking a lamp from the table we entered a vault where there were disposed in regular lines several coffers which he opened. They were full of gold and gems of every kind. *"You* see my son that with this one never fears poverty. Everything is yours; I am reaching the end of my career, and I shall be happy to leave them in your possession. These treasures are not the fruit of avarice and a sordid interest. I own them by the knowledge of Occult Sciences with which I am familiar and the boon which has been granted to me by The Great Being to penetrate the secrets of Nature. I can still command the Powers that populate the Earth and Space and are not visable to ordinary men.

"I like you, my dear son. I recognise in you the candour, sincerity, love of truth, and aptitude for these sciences, and most of all I wish you to know that they have cost me more than eighty years of research, meditation, and experience.

"The science of the Magicians, the language of the hieroglyphics, have been lost by the downfall of man.

Only I am the guardian. I will impart these precious confidences to you, and we will read together these characters traced on the pyramids which have been the despair of scholars and before which they have paled for many centuries."
The prophetic manner in which he spoke impressed me and I showed a very lively desire to understand that with which he wished to acquaint me. I told him this in the Turkish language which I was beginning to understand and to talk in a manner so that I could be understood.

"Your wishes shall be fulfilled," answered my adopted father. Then lifting one hand to the arch of heaven, he spoke in a solemn tone: Love, my son, love the very good and the very grand God of the philosophers, and never become proud if he brings you in contact with the children of wisdom for you to associate in their company and to make you a participant in the wonders of his power.

After having finished this invocation of sorts, he then said while looking at me: "Such are the principles which you must fathom. Try and make yourself worthy to receive the light. The hour of your regeneration has come. You will become like a new individual.

"Pray fervidly to Him who alone has the power to create new hearts, to give you that which will make you capable of great things that I have to teach you, and to inspire me to withhold from you none of the mysteries of Nature. Pray. Hope. I eulogise the eternal wisdom which has been placed in my soul and wish to disclose to you its ineffable truths. And you will be lucky, my son, if nature has placed in your soul the resolution that these high mysteries will demand of you. You will learn to command all Nature.

God alone will be your master, and the enlightened Will alone be your equal. The supreme intelligences will glory in obeying your desires. The Demons will not dare to be found where you are. Your voice will make them tremble in the pits of the abyss, and all the invisibles who inhabit the four elements will esteem themselves happy to administer to your pleasures. I adore you oh Great God for having enthroned man with so much glory, and having established him as sovereign monarch of all the works made by your hands.

"Do you feel, my son, do you feel this heroic ambition which is the sure stamp of the children of wisdom? Do you dare to desire to serve only the one God and to dominate over all that is not God? Have you understood what it is to prove to be a man and to be unwilling to be a slave since you are born to be a Sovereign? And if you have these noble thoughts, as the signs which I have found on your physiognomy do not permit me to doubt, have you considered maturely whether you have the courage and the strength to renounce all the things which could possibly be an obstacle to attaining the greatness for which you have been born?"

At this point he stopped and regarded me fixedly as if waiting for an answer, or as if he were searching to read my heart.

I asked him, "What is that which I have to renounce?"

"All that is evil in order to occupy yourself only with that which is good. The proneness with which nearly all of us are born to vice rather than to virtue. Those passions which render us slaves to our senses which prevent us from applying ourselves to study, tasting its sweetness, and gathering its fruits. You see, my dear son, that the sacrifice which I demand of you is not painful and is not above your powers; on the contrary, it will make you approach perfection as near as it is possible for man to attain. Do you accept that which I propose?"

"Oh my Father," I answered, "nothing conforms more to my desires that that one should choose propriety and virtue."

"It suffices," answered the old man. "Before unfolding to you completely the doctrine which will initiate you into the mysteries, which are most profound and the most sacred, you must understand that the elements are inhabited by very perfect creatures. The immense space between heaven and earth has inhabitants far more noble than the birds and the gnats. The vast seas have many other hosts than the whales and dolphin. It is the same in the depths of the earth which contains other things than water and minerals, and the element of fire, more noble than the other three, has not been created to abide there useless and empty. The air is full of an unnumbered multitude of beings with human form—a little proud in appearance but in effect docile and great lovers of the sciences; subtle but obliging to the great Mages and enemies of the foolish and the ignorant: these are the sylphs. The seas and rivers are the habitat of the Undines, the earth is full practically to the center of Gnomes, guardians of the treasures and the precious stones. These are the ingenious friends of man and easy to command. They supply to the children of the Magicians all moneys of which they have need and only ask payment for their services in the glory of being commanded. "As for the Salamanders, the inhabitants of the fire regions, they serve the philosophers, but they do not seek the attention of their company.

"I could also talk about the familiar spirits: Socrates, as well as Pythagoras and a few other wise men, had his. I have one also; he is near me when I have need of him. This will no doubt seem strange to you, but even if your eyes do not convince you of the truth, you will be able to believe it if you have any confidence in Socrates, Plato, Pythagoras, Zoroaster, Proclus, Porphyry, Iamblichus, Ptolemy, Trismegistus and other wise men to whose enlightenment one must add those who give us the natural knowledge.

"It remains for me to speak to you of the Talismans, those magic circles, which will give you the power to command all the elements, to avoid all the dangers, all the snares of your enemies, and to assure you the success of all your enterprises and the fulfillment of your wishes."

He arose, opened a chest which was at the foot of his bed, and took out a cedarwood box covered in gold veneer and enriched with diamonds of an extraordinary brilliance. The lock on which was engraved hieroglyphic characters was also of gold. He opened this casket, and I saw a large quantity of talismans and rings which were enriched with diamonds and engraved with magical and cabalistic symbols. It was impossible to look at them without being dazzled.

"You see, my son, each one has its virtue, its peculiar virtue, but to make use of it you must understand the language of the Magicians in order to pronounce the mysterious words engraved thereon. I will teach them to you before working with you on the great performance with the spirits and the animals who are submissive to my authority and who obey me blindly.

'You will see when you have been initiated into all these mysteries of how many errors the majority of those who pretend to be servile to nature have been guilty. They love the truth and believe they have discovered it by means of abstract ideas and lose their way in the faith of a reason of which they do not know the limits.

"The vulgar or common people do not see over the world in which they live other than an arch of glittering light during the day and a scattering of stars during the night. These are the limited ones of the universe. Certain of the philosophers have seen more and have increased (their knowledge) up to nearly the present time to the point of affrighting our imagination. Further, what prodigious work is offered at one stroke to the human spirit! Employ eternity even to survey it; take the wings of dawn, fly to the planet Saturn in the skies which extend over this planet. You will find without ceasing new spheres, new orbs, worlds accumulating one above another. You will find infinity in matter, in space, in movement, in the number of nuances and shades which adorn them. As our souls expand with our ideas and assimilate in a certain manner the objects which they penetrate, how much then must a man become elated at having penetrated the inconceivable profundities. I am an upstart thanks to wisdom, and you will reach this point too." He arose and took up several manuscripts which were on the table. "These precious books, my dear son, will acquaint you with things unknown to the rest of humanity and which will seem never to have existed. These books escaped the fire of the library of Ptolemy. They have received some damage, as you see; in effect, several pages have been blackened by the fire. "Ah well! It is by the knowledge which I have been able to draw from these works that I have the authority to command all the beings who inhabit the aerial and terrestrial regions, known and unknown to man.

"Oh my son! Prostrate yourself before the Divinity, deplore in His presence the errors of the human spirit, and promise Him to be as virtuous as it is possible for a man to be. Guard against studying moral philosophy in the ignorant writings of the multitudes, in the schemes produced by the heat of the imagination, by the restlessness of the spirit, or by the desire for celebrity which torments their authors.

Seek guidance in those works where, having no other interest than truth or other aim than public usefulness, they render to morals and to virtue the homage which they have deserved in all times and from all peoples."

I listened to this good old man with an admiration mixed with respect; he had stopped speaking and I thought I heard him still. A sweet majesty reigned in all his features, and the persuasion seemed to pour from his lips like a limpid stream running down a slope to fertilize the prairies. He noticed my admiration which was akin to ecstacy.

"My dear son," he said, "I pardon your astonishment. You have until now lived in the society of men who are corrupt, who have learnt to doubt everything and to forget the respect which one owes to Him who has brought forth all from nothing. Wisdom for them a meaningless difficulty, but as you learn it, it will become for you a practical virtue. You will look on it as something very simple, as natural to you as the air you breathe and as necessary to you for your existence. Your wounds are healing. Tomorrow I will commence your education in wisdom, and I will give you the first lesson. I am now going to my aviary to feed my prisoners."

"What!", I said to him. "Your prisoners! With your philosophy and the love of humanity which characterizes you, do you deprive living creatures of their liberty?"

He smiled at my observation. "My dear son, that which I do is necessary to facilitate my mysterious operations, but the destiny of those submissive to my laws is perhaps sweeter than if they enjoyed complete liberty. Besides, they have never known the prize and so cannot desire it. Tomorrow you will have the answer to all these enigmas.

He then left me to enter the cave where he had led me when he showed me the chests filled with gold and precious stones. Soon he came back. I got up. He told me to approach the awning so that we could eat something before going to sleep. He picked up the papers that were on the table. He took a seat and told me to sit by his side. I obeyed, but as I did not see any food, he laughingly added that this food was not very substantial but that in a moment I would see that he had cooks and slaves equally clever and intelligent. He immediately pronounced these words: Ag, Gemenos, Tur, Nicophanta, and blew three times on a ring which he had on his finger. Immediately the place was lit up by seven chandeliers of rock crystal which appeared from the void. Nine slaves entered bringing various viands on golden plates and wine in vessels of the greatest richness. Incense burned in tripods, and celestial music could be heard.

Everything was placed on the table in the most beautiful order, and the slaves stood to attention around us to serve.

"You see, my son," the good old man repeated to me, "I have but to command to be obeyed. Eat, serve yourself, and choose what will gratify you."

Everything which I tasted was delicious. Then I took my goblet, and the wine, like nectar, which had been poured into it, its bouquet forefunner to its delicate taste, appealed agreeably to my sense of smell.

When it had astonished my pallet and I had relished it, it seemed as though a divine fire flowed through my veins and as if I had acquired a new existence. I looked at the slaves who served us; they were all in the flower of their youth, of the greatest beauty, and dressed in rose silk tunics with white belts. They had flowing golden curls waving on their shoulders. With lowered eyes of respect, they attended to the orders of their master.

The old man allowed me to finish my survey, and he then followed up with: "My son you have appeased your hunger?" "Yes, my Father." He raised his hand and said: Osuam, Bedac, Acgos, and the slaves hurried to remove all that was on the table. They went out, the chandeliers disappeared, and two beds arranged themselves on each side of the apartment which was no longer lit except for the lamp that cast a soft light not unlike twilight.

"There, my dear son, is the manner in which you will be served every day. Your occupations will vary innumerably and thus will preserve you from tediousness. Deliver yourself to sleep, I will do the same, and tomorrow when day appears, I will keep my word which I have given to you."

"But my Father, the daylight will never penetrate into your abode; how can you know when break of day will appear?"

"That depends on my will, my son; it is another surprise that I will arrange for you. Until tomorrow, sleep in peace."

He extended his hand to me, and I pressed it to my heart. He approached his bed, lay down and soon sleep weighed down his eyes. I imitated him for a little while after which I fell asleep.

Then I opened my eyes the lamp had vanished, daylight lit the chamber, and the rays of sun penetrated there. The old man was walking with a book in his hand. The movement that I made interrupted his perusal. He looked at me smilingly. I got up hurriedly and flew into the arms he opened to me.

"My father, I salute you."

"You have rested well, my dear son," he said, as I judge by the calm which reigns on your countenance. Render homage to God who has permitted you to enjoy again this beautiful day, which lights you, and ere I initiate you into the mysteries of wisdom, I will have a conversation with you on a point of my doctrine which is necessary for developments." He gave me a book and opening it said: "Here is the first page and the prayer which you must address to the Great Being." And I read that which follows:

ORATION OF THE SAGES

Immortal, Eternal, Ineffable, and Sacred Father of all things, who is carried on the chariot rolling without cease, of the worlds which rotate always. Ruler of the Etheric Plain where Your throne of power is exalted and from whose heights Thy formidable eyes discover everything and Your beautiful and saintly ears hear everything. Harken to Your children whom You have loved from their birth through all time.

Since Your lasting, great, and eternal majesty shines brightly over the world and the starry heavens, Thou art raised above them. Oh, sparkling fire! There You light and maintain Yourself in the appropriate splendour. There comes forth from Your being never-failing streams of light which nourish Your infinite spirit. This infinite spirit generates all things and makes this inexhaustible treasure of matter which cannot fail to procreate that which always surrounds it because of the forms without number with which it is filled and with which You have filled it since the beginning of time. From this spirit the very saintly kings who are standing around Your throne and who compose Your court also draw their origin. Oh, Universal Father! Oh, Unique One! Oh, Father of blissful mortals and immortals! You have particularly created the powers which are marvelously like Your eternal thought and Your adorable essence. You have established them superior to the angels who announce Your wishes to the world. Finally, You have created us sovereigns over the elements. Our continued exertion is to praise You and to adore Your desires. We burn with the desire to be possessed of You. Oh, Father! Oh, Mother, the most tender of Mothers! Oh, admirable example of tender sentiments of Mothers! Oh, Son, the flower of all Sons! Oh, mould of all our shapes! Well beloved spirit, soul, harmony, and number of all things, we adore You.

When I had finished, he said to me: "My dear son, I have spoken to you of the spirits that populate the firmament, the sea, the earth, and fire, that is to say the elements. I have spoken to you of the spirits and am going to go into greater detail to extend the limits of your intelligence and to give you the means of penetrating into and understanding the sacred mysteries which will be divulged to you.

"When the universe was full of life, this unique son, this God-engendered, had received a spherical body, the most perfect of all; he was subject to circular movement, the simplest of all, the most suitable to his shape. The Supreme Being surveyed his work with complaisance, and having compared it with the model which He followed in his operations, He recognised with pleasure that the principal traits of the original repeated themselves in the copy. He did not grant him eternity for these two worlds could not have the same perfections. He made time, the mobile image of immobile eternity, which measures the duration of the sensible world as eternity measures that of the intellectual world, and for that He left traces of his presence and his movements. The Supreme Being kindled the sun and cast him with the other planets into the vast solitude of the airs. It is from there that this heavenly body floods the sky with its light.

The contriver of all things then addressed His commandment to the spirits to whom he had entrusted the administration of the heavenly bodies.

"Gods, who owe your birth to Me, listen to My sovereign commands. You do not have the right to immortality; but you participate in it by the power of My will, more powerful than the bonds which unite the parts of which you are composed. It remains for the perfection of all this to fill with inhabitants the seas, the earth, and the airs. If they should owe the day to Me immediately, escape the empire of death, they would become equal to the gods themselves. I thus lay on you the care of producing them. Agents of My power, unite to these perishable bodies the favor of immortality which you have received from My hand. Mold in particular those beings who command other animals and who are submissive to you; who are born by your orders; who increase by your good deeds, and who after their death are reunited with you and participate in your happiness."

He spoke, and suddenly, pouring into the basin where he had kneeded the Soul of the World the remainder of this Soul held in reserve, he then fashioned the individual Souls, and joining to those of men a small portion of the Divine Essence, he attached to them irrevocable destinies. Finally, having appointed to the inferior gods the successive reclothement of mortal bodies to provide for and control their needs, the Supreme Being re-entered into eternal rest. The inferior gods were obliged to employ the same means in developing us and thus the maladies of the body and the even more dangerous ones of the soul. All that is good in the universe in general and in man in particular derives from the Supreme God; all that is defective comes from the vices inherent in matter.

"The earth and the heavens are populated, my dear son, with Spirits to whom the Supreme Being has confided the administration of the Universe; He has distributed them everywhere nature appears to be animated but principally in those regions which stretch around and above us from the earth up to the sphere of the Moon. It is there where an immense authority is exercised, they dispensing life and death, the good and the bad, light and darkness.

"Each nation, each individual finds in these invisible representatives an ardent friend to protect him, an enemy no less ardent to pursue him. They are clothed in an aerial body; their essence holds the middle between Divine Nature and nature; they surpass us in intelligence; some of them are subject to our passions, mostly in the changes which pass them on to a superior rank. Because of their innumerable multitude, spirits are divided into four classes: the first of perfect beings whom the common herd adore and who reside in the stars; the second, those of the spirits properly called and of whom I conversed with you; the third, those beings less perfect who however, render great service to humanity; the fourth, those of our souls, after they have been separated from the bodies which they inhabited. We may discern from the first three the honors which will one day become part of our nature if we cultivate exclusively wisdom and virtue.

"To render you more sensible of that which I have put forward to you relative to the spirits, I will give you an account of what befell me with those who are submissive to me. Know also that they only communicate to souls after a long time of preparation in meditation and prayer. The dominion which I have obtained over my spirit is the result of my constancy in the practice of the virtues. In the beginning I saw him only rarely; one day yielding to my repeated entreaties he transported me to the realm of the spirits. Listen, my son, to the story of my voyage.

'The moment of departure having arrived, I felt my soul detatch itself from the bonds which attached it to the body, and I found myself in the middle of a new world of animated substances, good or malignant, blithe or sad, prudent or careless. We followed them for some time, and I thought I recognized some who were directing the interests of nations and those of individuals, the researches of sages and the opinions of the multitude.

"Soon a woman of gigantic stature extended her black veils over the vault of the skies; and having descended slowly to earth, she gave her orders to the cortege which had accompanied her. We glided into several houses. Sleep and its ministers scattered poppies with full hands; and while silence and peace spread gently around virtuous men, remorses and frightful spectres shook the beds of the wicked with violence.

"'Dawn and the hours open the barriers of the day,' my guide said to me. 'It is time to rise into the air. See the tutelary spirits of Egypt soaring over the different towns and regions which the Nile irrigates. They dispel as much as possible the evils with which they are menaced; nevertheless, their countryside will be devastated because the spirits enveloped in dark clouds are advancing and thundering against us; he then announced to me the arrival of the army of which you formed a part because he had knowledge of its comming. 'Observe now these assiduous agents, who, with a flight as rapid and as restless as the swallow, skim over the earth and cast piercing looks on all sides for greed and avidity; these are the inspectors of human affairs. Some spread their sweet influence over the mortals whom they protect; others launch the relentless Nemesis against grave transgressions. See these mediators, these expounders who rise and descend without cease; they carry your prayers and your offerings to the gods; they bring back to us happy or distressing dreams and the secrets of the future which are then revealed to you by the mouth of the oracles.'

"Oh my protector!" I cried suddenly, "here are beings which in their stature and sinister appearance inspire terror; they come to us.

"'Flee,' he said to me, 'they are unhappy, the good fortune of others irritates them, and they spare only those who pass their life in sufferings and in tears.'

"Escaping from their fury, we found objects no less afflicting. Discord, the detestable and eternal source of dissentions which torment men, marched proudly above their heads and whispered outrage and vengeance into their hearts. With timid steps and lowered eyes, the prayers trailed on their steps and endeavoured to recall everywhere the calm they had showed themselves. Glory was pursued by envy who tore her own sides; truth by impos re who changed its face from moment to moment; each virtue by several vices which carried snares or knives.

"Fortune appeared suddenly. My guide said to me, 'You can speak with her.' I felicitated her on the gifts which she distributed to mortals. She told me in a serious tone that she did not give but took a great interest. While uttering these words, she soaked the flowers and fruits which she held in one hand in a poisoned cup which she held in the other.

"Then passed near us two powerful spirits who left long trails of light after them. The one was war and the other wisdom.

"My guide told me two armies were approaching each other and were on the point of coming to blows. Wisdom would place herself near the general whose cause was just and he would be the victor because worth must triumph.

"'Let us leave these unhappy spheres,' said my spirit. We leapt the limits of the sphere of darkness and death with the speed of lightning and of thought. We then shot above the sphere of the Moon, and we reached the regions lit by eternal day. 'Let us stop for an instant,' said my guide. 'Cast your eyes over the magnificent spectacle which surrounds you; listen to the divine harmony which is produced by the regular movement of the celestial bodies; look how to each planet, each star, is attached a spirit which directs its course. These heavenly bodies are populated by sublime intelligences of a nature superior to ours.

'With my eyes fixed on the sun, I contemplated with ravishment the spirit who with a vigorous arm pushes this scintillating globe on the course which he has decreed. I watched him cast aside with fury the souls who endeavoured to plunge into the boiling surges of this sphere to purify themselves although they were not worthy of this blessing. Touched by their misfortune, I begged my conductor to take me away from this sight and to lead me into the distance towards an enclosure where one could escape the rays of light which were too brilliant. I hoped to catch a glimpse of the Sovereign of the Universe surrounded by the assistants of His throne and of those pure beings who our philosophers call numbers, eternal ideas or spirits of the mortals. My spirit told me that the Sovereign inhabits regions inaccessable to humans, that we should offer him our homage and descend to earth.

"Hardly had he spoken when we found ourselves in the same place from whence we had made our departure. He said to me, 'I have let you become acquainted with that which no mortal has ever been permitted to glimpse. From this moment it is no longer forbidden to me to hide anything from you.' And he unveiled to me all the mysteries in which I will let you participate. To convince you of the truth of all that I have given out to you, you will see my spirit, who will become yours since I have adopted you as my son. He will see in you another me.'

He pronounced these two words: Koux, Ompax. In that instant I saw appear a young man of the most beautiful stature; the remainder of his person shone with all the charms, and on the summit of his head shone a flame of which my eyes could not sustain the brilliance. He said smiling at the old man: Oles, Nothos, Perius. The old man took his hand and answered: Solathas, Zanteur, Dinanteur. The spirit took his place by his side.

The old man noticed that the spirit's light dazzled my eyes. "When you have been initiated into the mysteries of wisdom, you will be able to contemplate this fire without danger and even to stand the rays of the sun. Let us begin the initiation, let us stand."

I executed this order which he had given as did the spirit. He placed his hand on my head and said:

"Sina, Misas, Tanaim, Orsel, Misanthos." A voice which came from the cavern wherein were the coffers containing all the precious stones gave this answer:

"Torzas, Elicanthus, Orbitau ." Hardly had the last word been pronounced than we found ourselves in the most profound darkness. The fire which shone on the head of the spirit had also disappeared.

"Be without dread or fear," the old man said.

"My father, am I not with you?"

"Your answer pleases me, it proclaims confidence. You will now test the effects of it." He then said:

"Thomatos, Benasser, Elianter." Everything was then lit up but by a seemingly dark light, and I saw enter several individuals who took up positions around the room. "Here are all the spirits who will be subservient to you; I will proclaim them to you." He took me by the hand and conducted me around the room. He stopped in front of every spirit and said to me, "Repeat with me: Litau, Izer, Osnas." I obeyed and each spirit bowed saying, "Nanther." There were thirty-three. When we had reached the last one, he told me to return to the place which I had occupied. Then he took a wand six feet in length having at one end the head of a serpent and at the other the tail. On the wand were plates of gold the same as the head and tail on which were engraved the characters as illustrated in Figure 1.

NO. 1

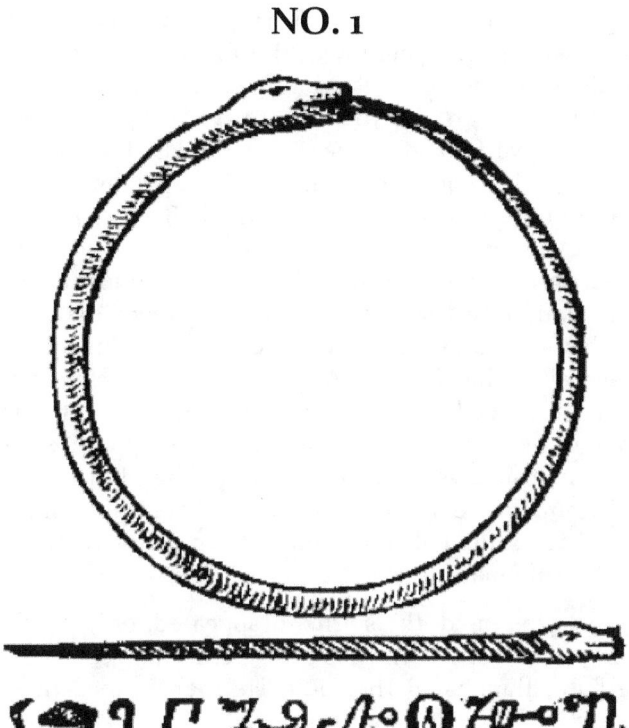

FIGURE OF THE WAND STAINED WITH BLOOD OF THE LAMB. THESE CHARACTERS SHOULD BE WRITTEN ON THE WAND WITH INDIA INK.

He formed a circle by uniting each end by a golden chain which he passed through two links; he put it on the ground and placed himself in the center. "What do you wish to see at this moment, my son?" he asked me.

"The plain on which you found me at the point of death from pain and want," I answered.

He raised his hands toward heaven and said, "Soutram, Ubarsinens." Immediately the spirits approached me and taking me in their arms, they lifted me, and I found myself transported to the foot of the Pyramid. I saw a multitude of Arabs on horseback who were surveying it. Although I had not noticed him, the old man was near me enjoying my astonishment. "You see, my son, how all the spirits are submissive to you, how they will obey you and await your orders. Do you wish to return to the place which you left or to soar for some time in the middle of the aerial parts? Do you know that you can see all that is happening around you and that you are visible only to the Great Being who wishes to accord you wisdom and to those who accompany you?" I testified to the desire to survey the immensity. "Pronounce Saram while extending your arms towards the east, and you will be satisfied." I uttered this word and made the indicated sign. The spirits lifted me up as well as the old man. We approached the clouds, and the vast horizon opened to my enchanted eyes. The old man once again said to me: "You see I have not made vain promises, you will have the same success in all your undertakings, but let us return to the Pyramid. The spirits await us, and we will continue our workings." He said "Rabiam," and very soon we re-entered the abode of the old man.

When we were seated, the spirits disappeared, only the first one remaining with us. All the insignia were changed, and a very intense light illuminated the vault. He then formed the second Magic Circle.

NO. 2

Placing himself therein, the old man said to me: "Go near your spirit. I give you permission for I know that you have a pure heart, that you have never been guilty of any action which would make you blush. If that were not the case, you would be struck down dead on entering this circle. Go, my son." I followed his instructions. He opened the casket where all the rings were to be found, and drew out that one shown in Figure 3 as well as the talisman which he placed in my hands.

NO.3

"This one will serve to conjur the celestial and infernal powers. Put the ring on your finger and the talisman over your heart, then pronounce the following words: Siras, Etar, Besanar, and you will perceive the effects."

Hardly had these words come from my mouth than I saw a multitude of spirits and figures of different shapes. The spirit who was at my side said to me: "Command and order and your desires will be satisfied." The old man added, "My son, the sky and the hells are at your orders. I think that at this moment you are not in want of anything; therefore, if you believe me, put off until later proving the Intelligence and activity of these spirits. To make them disappear, remove the ring from your finger and the talisman from the place which it occupies, and they will return to their sphere." I did that which he ordered me to do, and they all went like a dream.

"There remain many things for me to teach you to make you at ease with these rings and talismans. This instruction will be the object of very important work which we shall do together with the help of our spirit.

"Let us follow the course of our experiences. Stay where you are." He gave me another ring and talisman (Figure No. 4).

NO.4

THESE CHARACTERS SHOULD BE ENGRAVED ON THE INSIDE OF THE RING.

"These two precious objects, my son, are destined to make you loved by the most beautiful portion of the human race. There is not a woman who would not be happy to please you and who would not employ all possible means to be successful at it. Do you wish the most beautiful odalisque of the Grand Caliph should be brought before you in an instant? Put the ring on the second finger of your left hand, press the talisman against your lips, and say tenderly in a whisper: o Nades, Suradis, Manier." Suddenly a spirit with rose-coloured wings appeared; he placed himself on his knees before me. "He awaits your orders," the old man said. "Say to him: Sader, Prostas, Solaster." I repeated these words, and the spirit vanished.

"He is going to traverse an immense space with the rapidity of thought, and the most beautiful forms will appear before your eyes and will serve as a model to paint those houris which our Divine Prophet promises to his faithful servants. O my son, how blessed you are; not every mortal obtains from the Great Spirit such favours as I can see by the speed with which your wishes are executed."

He had finished speaking when the spirit with the rose-coloured wings arrived carrying in his arms a woman enveloped in a large white veil. She seemed to be asleep, and he placed her gently on a couch which appeared near me. He raised the veil which hid her. Never had anything so beautiful been offered to my eyes; she was Venus with all the charms of innocence. She sighed and opened the most beautiful eyes in the world which came to rest on meo In a most harmonious voice she uttered a cry of surprise saying, "It is he." The old man told me to approach the beauty, place a knee on the ground, for it is thus that one should speak to her, and to take her hand. I obeyed, and the divinity to whom I addressed my homage said to me: "I have seen thee in a dream, and the reality thereof makes thee more dear to my heart. I prefer you to the Sultan who for a long time has fatigued me with his homage." "That is enough," said the old man, and he said forcefully, "Mammes Laher." Four slaves appeared to remove the couch and she who had made such a vivid impression on my heart. The old man noticed my emotion and the pain which resulted from her departure. He said to me, "You will see her again. Understand that in order to possess wisdom, it is necessary to know how to resist the allurements of voluptuousness."

His words made me come to myself, and I said to him, "Pardon, my father, but you have seen her, that is my excuse."

I replaced the ring and the talisman in the casket, and he gave me that which is illustrated in Figure No. 5.

NO.5

THESE CHARACTERS SHOULD BE ENGRAVED ON THE INSIDE OF THE RING.

"This talisman and this ring are not less valuable. They will enable you to discover all the treasures which exist and to ensure you the possession of them. Place the ring on the second finger of your right hand, enclose the talisman with the thumb and little finger of your left hand, and say, Onaim, Perantes, Rasonastos." I repeated these three words, and seven spirits of a bronze colour appeared, each carrying a large hide bag which they emptied at my feet. They contained gold coins which rolled in the middle of the hail where we were. I had not noticed that one of the spirits had on his shoulder a black bird, its head covered with a kind of hood. "It is this bird," the old man said to me, "who has made them find all this treasure. Do not think that these are some of what you have seen here. You can assure yourself of this." I replied, "You are for me the truth itself. My father! Do you believe that I would insult you by doubting?"

He made a sign, and the spirits replaced the gold in the bags and disappeared.

"You see, my son, what the virtues of these talismans and rings are. When you know them all, you will be able, without my aid, to perform such miracles as you judge proper. Replace in the casket those of which you have made proof, and take this one (Figure No. 6).

NO.6

THESE CHARACTERS SHOULD BE ENGRAVED ON THE INSIDE OF THE RING.

"They will enable you to discover the most hidden secrets; you will be able to penetrate everywhere without being seen, and not a single word in the universe can be uttered without it coming to your ears, whether you wish to listen to it yourself or to have it brought back to us by your agents when you order them to do so. To prove it to you, repeat these words and place the talisman near your ear while you hold the ring tightly in your left hand: Nitrae, Radou, Sunandam." I distinctly heard a voice which said to me: "The Grand Mogul has decided in his private council that he must declare war on the Emperor of China." Another voice said to me: "All is rumour in Constantinople. Last night the Sultana was carried off, and the Grand Sultan is in despair. He has had all the eunuchs thrown into the sea after having had them beheaded." "Oh Heavens! What mischief I have done without wishing it," I cried in pain. "Well, my son," the old man said, "it is a lesson for you to learn— not to be enslaved by your passions and to know how to curb them. This is enough for today, tomorrow we will continue."

The next day we followed the course of our mysterious operations. The spirit had not left us. "You see, my son," said the old man, "that everything becomes easy with confidence and a pure soul without stain."

He opened the casket and took from it the talisman and ring (Figure No. 7).

NO.7

THESE MAGICAL CHARACTERS SHOULD BE ENGRAVED ON THE INSIDE OF THE RING.

When he had placed them in my hands, he pronounced two words, which I will teach you. "Place this ring on the little finger of your left hand and the talisman to your right ear, and the most discreet man will divulge to you his most hidden thoughts. Here are the two words: Noctar, Raiban, and if you add a third word, which is Biranther, your greatest enemies will not be able to prevent themselves from loudly publishing their projects against you. In order to convince you, I am going to have appear before you one of the Beys of Cairo, and he will impart to you all of his schemes against the French." He then said

"Nocdar," to the spirit who then vanished like lightening. A quarter of an hour after he returned with the Bey who said: "We have made a treaty of alliance with the English, and the armistice concluded with the French will be broken without warning." He disappeared with the spirit after the old man had said:

"Zelander. The Mufti of the Grand Mosque will appear before your eyes and show you a manuscript of a work which he has composed and which he has refused to show to his best friends, even the Grand Visir." I did that which has previously been indicated, and very soon the Mufti appeared and placing his manuscript on the table, he said to me: "Tonas, Zugar," which means in the language of the magi: read and believe. The old man looked at him affectionately; he gave him his hand pronounced with sweetness and expression, o Solem. The Mufti, after bowing, disappeared.

"Return the talisman and the ring to me," the old man said, "and take this." (Figure No. 8)

NO.8

CHARACTERS TO BE ENGRAVED ON THE INSIDE OF THE RING.

"It will serve to activate as many spirits as you wish to undertake or to stop operations which would be contrary to you. The magic words are: Zorami, Zaitux, Elastot. We will not at this moment make any experiments; tomorrow we will go to the shores of the Nile and we will have constructed a bridge of a single arch on which we shall pass to the other side of the river.

"Here is the next talisman and its ring (Figure No. 9).

NO. 9

THESE CHARACTERS SHOULD BE ENGRAVED ON THE INSIDE OF THE RING.

They have the property of destroying everything, of commanding the elements, of calling down the thunder, hail, the stars, earthquakes, hurricanes, water spouts on land and sea, and of preserving our friends from all accidents. Here are the words which one must pronounce (the numbers indicate each thing that you wish to operate): first, you pronounce: Ditau, Hurandos; second, Ridas, Talimol; third, Atrosis, Narpida; fourth, Uusur, Itar; fifth, Hispen, Tromador; sixth, Paranthes, Histanos.

"The talisman and the ring (Figure No. 10) will make you invisible to all eyes, even those of the spirits.

NO.10

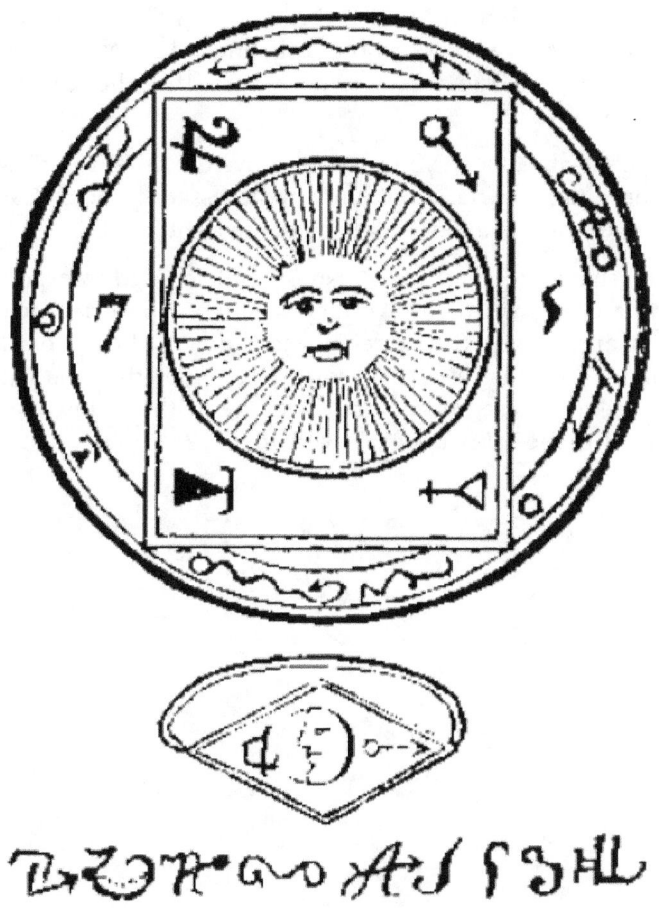

CHARACTERS TO BE ENGRAVED ON THE INSIDE OF THE RING.

Only the Great Being could be witness to your steps and your actions. You will penetrate everywhere into the bosom of the seas, into the bowels of the earth, you can likewise survey the airs, and no action of men can be hidden from you. Say only: Benatir, Cararkau, Dedos, Etinarmi."

I repeated these four words, and through the walls of the Pyramid I saw two Arabs who were on the plain and who were profiting by the obscurity to ransack a tomb where they hoped to find something of value.

"You will be able, when you wish, to prove the other things which I will have taught you, it will only be necessary to place the ring successively on the different fingers of the right hand.

"The talisman and ring (Figure No. 11) will serve to transport you into whatever part of the world you judge appropriate without running any danger. Say merely these words: Raditus, Polastrien, Terpandu, Ostrata, Pericatur, Ermas. But I hope that you will not make use of these means to leave me without my consent. Promise it to me." "My father, I swear to it."

NO.11

CHARACTERS TO BE ENGRAVED ON THE INSIDE OF THE RING.

"With the talisman and the ring (Figure No. 12) you will be able to open all locks, no matter what secrets have been employed to shut them; you will not need a key. Simply by touching them with the ring and pronouncing these three words: Saritap, Pernisox, Ottarim, they will open of themselves without difficulty. Make proof of this on the spot, my son," the old man told me. "Close the casket which you see on that table." I did this, and after having assured myself that nothing could open it but the key, I touched it with the ring and pronounced the magic words, and it opened of its own accord. "It will be the same," added the old man, "with all the doors of prisons, fortified castles, where they might lock you up.

NO.12

CHARACTERS TO BE ENGRAVED ON THE INSIDE OF THE RING.

"With the talisman and ring (Figure No. 13), you will be able to see what takes place in all houses without being obliged to enter them; you will be able to read the thoughts of everyone whom you approach and with whom you find yourself, and you will be able to render them service or do them injury as you wish. It will be sufficient to place the talisman on your head and then to blow on the ring saying: o Tarot, Nizael, Estarnas, Tantarez these words are for knowing the thoughts of people.

"In order to render service to those who deserve it, you say: Nista, Saper, Visnos, and they will immediately enjoy all sorts of prosperities.

"To punish the wicked and your enemies, you will say: Xatros, Nifer, Roxas, Rortos, and they will at once suffer punishment and frightful torment. What you have already seen should prove to you that I have advanced nothing which cannot be realised; therefore it is useless to make proof thereof.

NO.13

CHARACTERS TO BE ENGRAVED ON THE INSIDE OF THE RING.

"The talisman and the ring (Figure No. 14) will serve you to destroy all the projects which could be made against you, and if

any spirit wished to oppose your wishes, you could force him to submit to you. Place the talisman on a table under your left hand and with the ring on the second finger of the right hand, you say in a bass voice, while inclining your head:
Senapos, Terfita, Estamos, Perfiter, Notarin.

NO.14

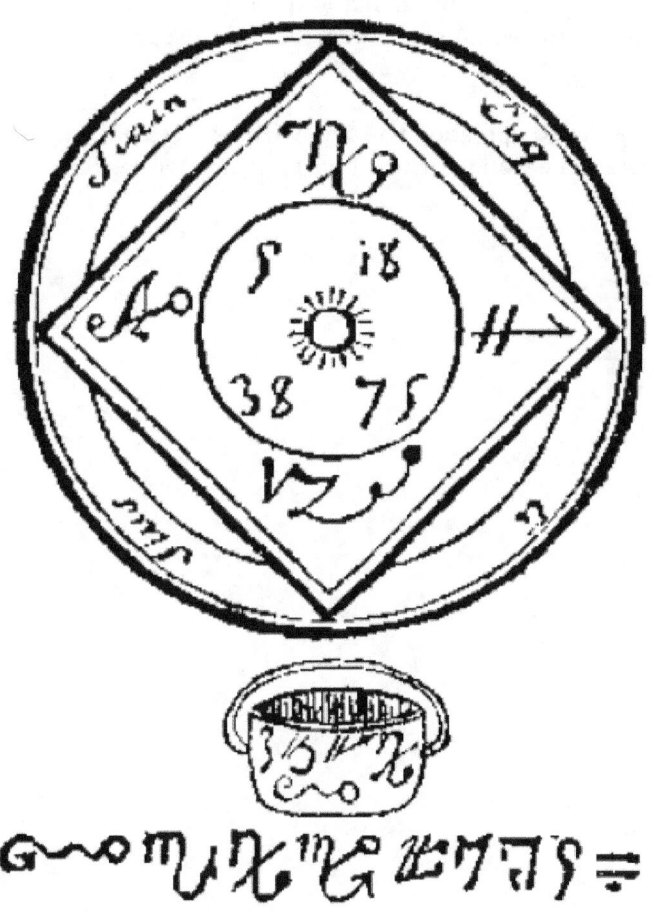

CHARACTERS TO BE ENGRAVED ON THE INSIDE OF THE RING.

"The talisman and ring (Figure No. 15) have a property as extraordinary as agreeable; they will give you all the virtues, all the talents, and the inclination to do good by changing all substances which are of a bad quality and rendering them excellent. For the first object, while elevating the talisman and with the ring placed on the first joint of the third finger of the left hand, it is sufficient to pronounce these words:

Turan, Estonos, Fuza.

"For the second operation you say: Vazotas, Testanar, and you will see operate the wonder which I have proclaimed to you.

NO.15

CHARACTERS TO BE ENGRAVED ON THE INSIDE OF THE RING.

"The talisman and the ring (Figure No. 16) will assist you to know all the minerals and vegetables, their virtues and properties, and you will possess the universal medicine. There is no illness that you will not be able to cure and no cure that you will undertake without success. Aesculapius and Hippocrates will only be novices compared to you. You pronounce only these words: Reterrem, Salibat, Cratares, Hisater, and when you are near a sick person you will carry thet talisman on the stomach and the ring with a St. Andrew's Cross around your neck on a ribbon the colour of fire.

NO.16

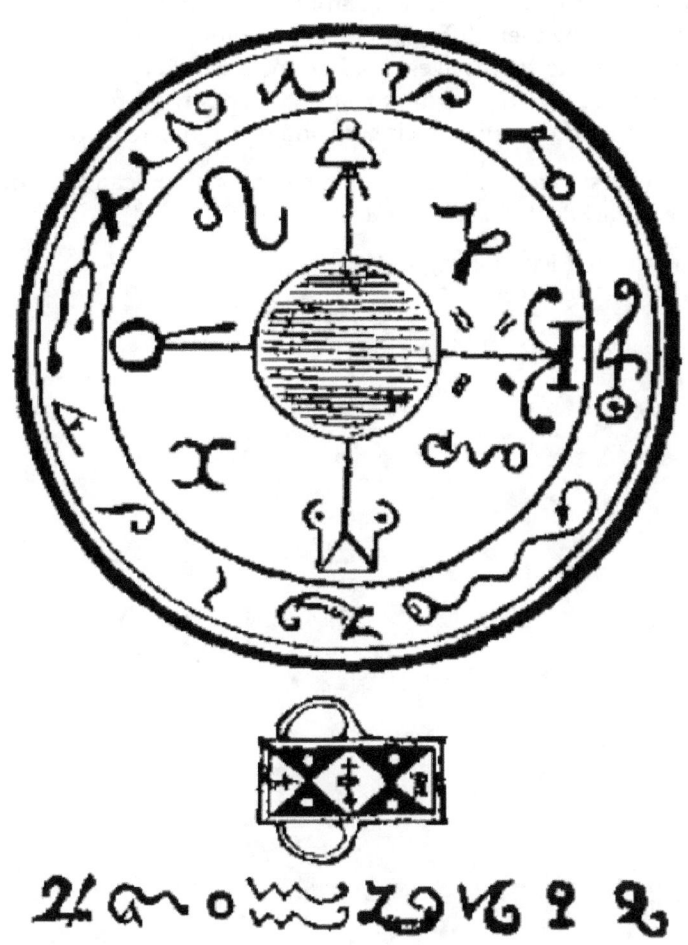

CHARACTERS TO BE ENGRAVED ON THE INSIDE OF THE RING.

"The talisman and the ring (Figure No. 17) will keep you safe in the midst of the most ferocious animals, to subdue them to your will, to know by their different cries what they want as they have a language among themselves. Mad animals will keep at a distance from you, and you will make them perish forthwith by pronouncing the words which I am going to indicate to you.

"For the first operation it is sufficient to say: Hocatos, Imorad, Surater, Markila. For the second:

Trumantrem, Ricona, Estupit, Oxa.

NO.17

CHARACTERS TO BE ENGRAVED ON THE INSIDE OF THE RING.

"The talisman and ring (Figure No. 18) will enable you to know the good or bad intentions of all the individuals whom you will meet to guarantee you of it and to impress on their face a mark which will be noticed by everyone. It is sufficient to pronounce these mysterious words, while placing the talisman on your heart and the ring on the little finger of your right hand. You will then say: Crostes, Furinot, Katipa, Garinos.

NO.18

CHARACTERS TO BE ENGRAVED ON THE INSIDE OF THE RING.

"The talisman and the ring (Figure No. 19) will give you all talents and a profound understanding of all the arts so that you can perform with as much brilliance as the greatest masters and foremost artists. It is sufficient to carry the talisman and the ring in a manner you judge suitable while pronouncing these seven words: Ritas, Onalun, Tersorit, Ombas, Serpitas, Quitathar, Zamarath while adding afterwards the name of the art or the talent which you wish to possess.

NO.19

"The talisman and the ring (Figure No. 20) will help you to win at lotteries and to make certain when playing a game that you will obtain the fortune of your adversaries. You will place the talisman on your left arm, adjusting it with a white ribbon, and the ring on the little finger of your right hand; then you will say these words: Rokes for a selection, Pilatus for a combination of two numbers, Zotas for dice, Tulitas for four winning numbers, Xatanitos for five winning numbers. Be sure to pronounce all the words when you are on a quine, and for a card game you will pronounce them each time the cards are shuffled, if it is you or your partner, and before commencing you will touch your left arm on the spot where the talisman is to be found with your right hand, and you will kiss your ring. All this must be done without drawing the attention of your adversary.

NO. 20

"The talisman and the ring (Figure No. 21) will enable you to direct all the infernal powers against your enemies or against those who would injure your friends. You will carry it in a manner which you consider suitable and pronounce merely these three words: Osthariman, Visantiparos, Noctatur.

NO.21

CHARACTERS TO BE ENGRAVED ON THE INSIDE OF THE RING.

"The talisman and the ring (Figure No. 22) will serve you to recognise what the infernal powers wish to undertake, and you can abort all their projects by placing the talisman on your chest and the ring on the first joint of the little finger of the left hand. You pronounce these words: Actatos, Catipta, Bejouran, Itapan, Marnutus.

NO.22

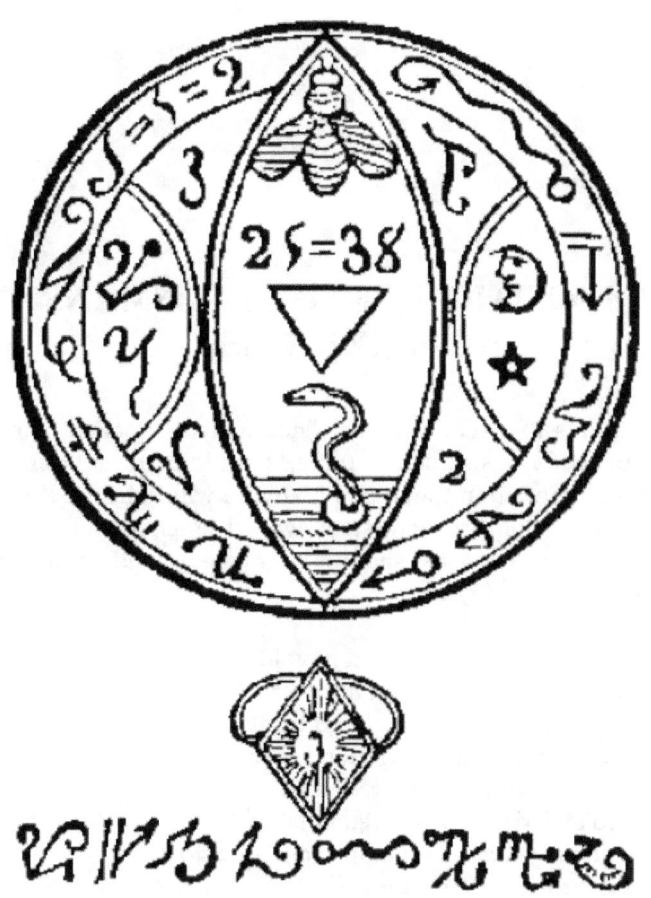

CHARACTERS TO BE ENGRAVED ON THE INSIDE OF THE RING.

COMPOSITION OF THE TALISMANS AND THE RINGS

"As it is possible that you have not had the means of making talismans and rings similar to mine," the old man said to me, "you will make them up in the manner which I will indicate. Know that the rings are of bronzed steel with the characters engraved thereon. The talismans should be made of silk cloth in the dimensions of the figures.

No. 1. White satin embroidered in gold.
No. 2. Red satin embroidered in silver.
No. 3. Sky-blue satin embroidered in silver.
No. 4. Black satin embroidered in silver.
No. 5. Green satin embroidered in gold.
No. 6. Violet satin embroidered in silver.
No. 7. Golden-yellow satin embroidered in gold.
No. 8. Lilac satin with shaded silk.
No. 9. Poppy-red satin embroidered in silver.
No. 10. Yellow satin embroidered in black silk.
No. 11. Puce satin embroidered in gold.
No. 12. Dark blue satin embroidered in silver.
No. 13. Pale grey satin embroidered in gold.
No. 14. Rose satin embroidered in silver.
No. 15. Golden-yellow satin embroidered in silver.
No. 16. Orange satin embroidered in silver.
No. 17. Dark green satin embroidered in gold.
No. 18. Black satin embroidered in gold.
No. 19. White satin embroidered in black silk.

No. 20. Cherry satin embroidered in silver.
No. 21. Grey-White satin, shaded.
No. 22. Red satin, embroidered in the middle with gold, the border in silver, and the signs in black and white silk.

The old man, after having given me this information, replaced all the talismans and rings in the casket.

The spirit who was at my side closed it arid gave him the key. The old man said to me: "All the wonders which have been performed in front of You, my dear son, ought not to leave any doubt of the Power and virtue of these talismans and rings. If you have not experienced any obstacle in your enterprises, it is because your heart is pure, that your soul is without stain, and that virtue, probity, and honour will always be dear to you. A man who had the least reproach to make to himself, who had destroyed the good of others, or who had only the intention of so doing, would not be able to participate in our mysteries. In vain would he have in his possession all that you see, our magical language known to him.

The celestial powers—aerial, infernal, terrestrial, and those of the oceans and fire—would rebel against him. All that he wished to undertake would turn to his shame and his confusion, and at each invocation which he might make, the powers that he implored for help and intervention would answer him: Renounce thy projects. Thou art guilty. Before commanding us, purify thyself, expiate thy faults.

"If after these emanations he continued to conjure the powers, he would finish by being punished and would without fail lose his life. Remember then, my dear son, that all is possible with virtue and that not one fault will remain unpunished. There are still two prayers which you must be careful to recite before and after each conjuration that you wish to do; here they are:

FIRST PRAYER

The Celestial Fire above is an incorruptable flame, always scintillating, the source of life, fountain of all the Beings, and principle of all things. This flame produces all and nothing perishes except which it consumes: it makes itself known by it-self. This fire cannot be contained in any place; it is without body or matter. It encompasses the skies, and from it emanates a little spark which makes all fire of the Sun, of the Moon, and the Stars. That is what I know of God: do not try to know more because that is beyond you, such judge as thou art. Moreover, know that the unjust or wicked man can-not hide himself in front of God; no address or any excuse can disguise anything from his piercing eyes. All is clear to God: God is everywhere.

SECOND PRAYER

There is in God as immense profundity of flame; the heart ought not, however, to fear to touch or to be touched by this adorable fire; it will not be consumed by this sweet fire, whose tranquil and perishable heat makes the union, harmony, and duration of the world. Nothing exists except by this fire which is God. No one has engendered it; it is without mother, it knows all, and no one is able to know anything of it. It is immovable in its projects and its name is ineffable. Here then is that which is God; because for us, who are his messengers, we are but a small part of God.

"You see, my son, that all the instructions that I give you have as a basis the respect which one owes to God, Who is the principle of all things and Whose ineffable and limitless goodness fills us to the brim each day with all His goodness, when we render ourselves worthy of it by our respect and our submission to His will and His immutable decree."

The old man after these short reflections said to me: "You have no doubt noticed, my son, that I have spoken to you about the birds to whom I was going to give food, and you have seen spirits who had one with them; when the pieces of gold were deposited at your feet, it was these birds who enabled them to discover it by their instinct and by the magical and cabalistic words which one pronounced. To procure these birds there are difficulties without number that one must conquer, and the profane, those who are not initiated into our mysteries, make useless efforts to obtain them. It is of the marvelous Black Hen that I am going to converse with you. The great Oromasis, father of Zoroaster, was the first who possessed one; it is from him that I possess the secret of calling them into existence, and here is the manuscript in which is contained the manner of hatching these birds who are as rare as precious." He opened for me at the same time this manuscript whose cover was a thin plate of gold covered with diamonds, rubies, topazes and sapphires whose brilliance it was impossible to bear. The paper was of a dazzling whiteness, and the hieroglyphic characters were traced by hand in rose-coloured ink.

"I will teach YOU to read in this book as I can," he said to me, "but let us occupy ourselves with the way to hatch the Black Hen and to procure the eggs which she will come forth." He took several pieces of aromatic woods such as aloes, cedar, or lemon, laurel, some root of Iris, and some roses whose leaves had been dried in the sun. (Translators note: the author distinctly states leaves, not petals.) He put the lot in a chafing-dish of gold. poured on top thereof balsamic oil of the purest essence, transparent gum, and having pronounced the words: Athas, Solinam, Erminatos, Pasaim, the sun-light penetrated the vault. He placed a glass on the chafing-dish. At the same moment that the sun's struck the glass, the perfumes and pieces of odorous wood which were in the dish burst into flame, the glass liquified, and an agreeable odor was diffused in the vault. Very soon nothing was left but cinders. The old man, who had not ceased to watch with the greatest attention, took a golden egg which been in a black velvet bag and which I had not noticed. He opened this egg, closed the burning cinders therein, and placed it then on a black cushion.

He covered it with a faceted rock-crystal bell; then, raising his eyes and his arms toward the vault, he cried: o Sanataper, Ismai, Nontapilus, Ertivaler, Canopistus. The sun seemed to dart its rays on this bell with still greater force and violence.

The bell became the colour of fire, the golden egg disappeared before my eyes, a thin vapour rose in the air, and I saw a little black pullet which stirred, got to its feet and clucked faintly. The old man extended one of his fingers to it, and it placed itself thereon. He then pronounced these two words: Binusas, Testipas, and the winged creature glided onto his breast. There," said the old man, "is the manner of procuring a Black Hen. In a few days it will be of ordinary size, and I will instruct it in front of you. You will see the instinct of this animal to discover the most hidden treasures and that the smallest particle of gold cannot escape it. Let us give thanks to the Great Being who has permitted us to penetrate these mysteries and to perform such prodigies and marvels. We will say together the two prayers recounted further back." After having fulfilled this duty, he said to me, "My son, this is enough. We will take a little rest." The sun had shone on us for some time. It disappeared, and its light was replaced by that of several chandeliers. The spirit, who had not left us, took a lyre, and accompanying himself he sang in the language of the magicians of the Eternal Power and the marvels of nature.

The old man listened with attention to the accents of the spirit. For myself I was enchanted, arid he smiled in observing me. "This is enough," he said to the spirit. "Before delivering ourselves to rest, I wish to show you the means of having a Black Hen without having recourse to those which I have used, for it would be difficult to obtain the perfumes and the other materials which I placed in the chaffing-dish if others than you or I wished to perform this great work. But if someday you find someone who is worthy of being initiated, here is the means which you should employ. Take an egg which you will expose at noon to the gleams of the sun, observing that it has not the least stain. Then you choose a hen as black as possible; if it has any feathers of another colour, you will pull them out. You will cover its head with a hood of black material in such a manner that it can-not distinguish anything. You will allow it the use of it's beak. Enclose it in a box lined also with black material, big enough to contain it, and place that in a room where daylight cannot penetrate. Be careful to bring it food only at night. When all these indispensible precautions have been taken, you will give it the egg to sit on, taking care that it is not disturbed by any noise. It all depends on the blackness of this hen, its imagination will be impressed with it, and at the proper time you will see hatched a hen which is completely black. But I repeat to you, is necessary that those who perform this shall be worthy by their wisdom and virtue to participate in these sacred and divine mysteries. For, if we are not able to read the hearts of men, it is not the same with the Great Spirit; all is known to him and he penetrates our most secret intentions and our most hidden thoughts. It is after that that He accords or refuses to us His favours and His gifts.

"Our sitting has been so long," he added, "that We must take some food before delivering ourselves to rest." He clapped his hands three times, and the Slaves, the spirits who had previously appeared, offered themselves again to my attention, and in an instant we had all the viands that could satisfy taste aroma, and the eyes. The meal was very gay; the old man annimated it by his sallies. The spirit was also of the party. I was as inspired, and I joined the conversation. At last sleep weighed down our eyes, and we left the table to taste its sweetness. The most agreeable dreams lulled me with their cheerful images, and when I awoke daylight lit up our abode. I did not see the old man or the spirit. I thought that they had gone out, and I abandoned myself to my reflections. The present assures me of the future, nothing could make me anxious. If fortune gives happiness, I said to myself, who will be happier than I. I cannot see any wish which will not be accomplished at once; my lot would be envied if it were known by the remainder of men. I want to be able to return to my country soon. As I followed up this idea, I heard a slight noise and saw the old man enter followed by the spirit. They approached me, both took me by the hand, and I left my bed of rest at once.

'You have rested well, my dear son," the old man said. "During your sleep I went out with the spirit to visit my birds, and I am going to make you acquainted with their talents. At the same instant he touched a spring which was in the wall, a section opened, and seven black birds which I recognised as hens were brought in in a cage by two black slaves. "These animals have a marvelous instinct for finding gold. You will be the judge." He placed several pieces of gold under the cushions, in the crevices of walls under the folds of his turban, then said to the slaves: Tournabos, Fativos, Almabisos. They opened the cage, uncovered the heads of the birds, and the hens came out and flew immediately in the different places where the gold was hidden. They picked up the pieces in their beaks and deposited them at the feet of the old man. He took these birds one after the other and carressed them. He said to me: "You see how tame they are; we will go out for a while on the plain; I have placed in the sand several pieces of gold. We will release our birds, and soon they will have discovered the treasure." He made a sign to the slaves who reclosed the birds in the cage we departed.

As soon as we had come out of the Pyramid for about five hundred paces onto the plain, he released the birds. They went a few paces; soon it seemed that their instinct indicated to them where the treasure was to be found. They flew in that direction, and all seven of them started scratching. They soon discovered the sacks, and one of them started to cackle; we approached and saw the sacks which the old man had hidden. I could not prevent myself from showing my surprise. "My son, you see that all is possible with the aid of God and his powerful protection." We took the sacks and re-entered the Pyramid.

He had the birds re-enclosed with the same precautions as were taken to let them out. He then said to me:

"Let us see what condition my new-born is in." He opened a little box lined with down in which he had enclosed it, and already feathers were beginning to appear. "A few more days," he said, "and it will be able to receive the first lessons. He replaced the box in its place. "Since we have been together," said the old man, "we have not gone out; we will make a little excursion into the country and wear the costume of the locality." The spirit covered his head with a turban and dressed completely like a Turk. I did the same, and we prepared to depart. Before leaving I saw the old man take a talisman and a ring. I remarked on it, and he told me that perhaps it might be necessary for us and that precaution was the mother of security. We then went our way and walked quietly for some time. The old man spoke to us of the changes which took place in the world from time to time, of the revolution of the stars and the planets.

He seemed to give notice to us and to fore-shadow things which would follow. All of a sudden a horde of Arabs pounced upon us with raised swords. The old man looked at them without fright, and he raised his hand; the brigands stopped. He pronounced the words prescribed for the talisman (Figure No. 10) and we became invisible. The astonished Arabs looked on all sides without seeing us. It is impossible to paint a picture of the astonishment of these villains. Their chief appeared astounded. The old man smiled. He pronounced the word Natarter in a loud voice, and they took flight with lightening rapidity. "Be calm," said the old man. "For a long time they will not dare to appear in this territory."

We continued walking for some time. The time passed with an extraordinary rapidity; the conversation of the old man was so varied, so instructive, that it was impossible to listen to him without being charmed by all that he said. "Let us return to our abode." After having pronounced these words, he looked at the sun and cried: "Brilliant star, image of the Divinity, thou who vivifies the earth and gives life to nature, receive my homage; may I ere I leave the earth constantly enjoy thy light."
"What has given birth to these somber ideas," I immediately cried. "Why do you think of leaving earth?"

"Ah, my son! Each day which passes, each that we take leads us towards the tomb. Lucky is the just man who can go to sleep in peace in the care of God to enjoy thereafter the rewards promised to virtue. Also, my son, do you believe that I do not concern myself with my last hour? At my age it is permitted to think of it, and I have always lived in a manner so as to be able to die without fear. I am 270 years old, and I have seen many things pass; I will pass also when my turn comes. And now enough of this matter. I see that I trouble you, and that is not my intention. Let us talk of other things.

"The talisman and ring (Figure No. 20) will furnish you with the means to win at lotteries. I wish also to indicate to you an infallible calculation to obtain the same advantages. It is really very simple. You take a game of piquet composed of thirty-two cards. You shuffle them, cut and extract nineteen cards one after the other commencing with that which is underneath. Take their numbers: know, the ace is 11, the king 4, the queen 3, the knave 2, and the other cards their numerical value. Add up the total. Then add the 30 or 31 days of the month in which you find yourself, your age, the day of your birth, that is to say, the first, second or third or such other day, and a date when you have proved something happy or agreeable: you add all these numbers, you take a third of it, and you place in the lottery the numbers which this addition has given you. You can be certain that these numbers will come out in totality or in part on the different wheels. For instance, if you find the numbers 13, 52, 73, you can take again 31, 25, 37, and the unities. This calculation is infallible. You can convince yourself. The number 30 is priviledged, and it is from this that all is calculated for 3 times 30 makes 90; it is from this that one does not wish to exceed this number in the lottery. It is the same with all games.

"The numbers which have 3 for a root are the most fortunate; odd is all. God, after having created the world and being occupied for six days in establishing the admirable order which exists, rested on the seventh, which is odd. Let us take God as an example and a model in all that we do and we will be assured in all that we undertake. You have noticed, my son, that odd numbers are the basis of all the mysterious operations into which I have initiated you."

We continued our route and arrived at the Pyramid. He opened the door, and we went down. Arriving in the hall, we sat down on a sofa which faced the table on which was the casket of the tasilmans. The old man replaced the one which had served to clear away the Arabs, and we remained in silence for some time.

The old man appeared tired. He reclined on the and soon he was asleep. I cast my eyes on his venerable figure, and I admired his serenity, Calmness spread over all his features. I remarked about this to the spirit who told me: "It is the image of his soul. I have obeyed him for more than a century. You cannot have any idea of his virtue, of his wisdom, of his goodness. His days are numerous, and all are marked by some good deed, of the unhappy he has rescued without their ever knowing who the being was who came to their help. If the eternal Soul who has created all should take the figure of a mortal, it is his which He would borrow. Is not the just man in effect the image of God on earth? Many have taken title, but how many have usurped it and merited little." After having pronounced these words, the spirit got up, knelt on the ground near the old man, and raising his hands and eyes towards heaven, said in a solemn tone which awed me:

"Eternal Spirit, Who hears me and Who reads heart, prolong the life of this virtuous man. Ensure that he adorns by his presence for a long time to come the earth which You enrich with Thy gifts, unless You have reserved for him near Thee a reward worthy of him."

The sentiments with which he expressed these words keenly moved me. Tears wet my eyes, and I fell on my knees as he had.

The old man awoke at this moment, and casting his eyes on us, he said to us with a smile, "What are you doing, my children?" I answered that we were praying to the Great Being to conserve our father for us.

"My good friends," answered the old man, "our life has a term set by Providence which we cannot extend: everything begins, everything must end; God alone is eternal. The only thing which can survive us is the memory of our virtues and the good examples which we have set. While like voyagers we can perceive the course of our destiny and what good or evil we have done as we have been more or less the slaves of our passions, happy is he who has been able to command himself and to distinguish the happiness which is praiseworthy from what is not. For myself, I have been happy enough; I made the distinction in the springtime of my life, and in the winter I taste the sweetness. I shall soon return into the bosom of Him who has created me; a dream announced it to me in my sleep. In a few hours my soul will leave its mortal remains and will rise towards the celestial regions."

"Oh heavens! my father," I cried, "what do you announce?"
"What you must await like myself, my dear son but I bless my departure since I have the consolation in dying of leaving my heritage to a man who is deserving, who loves virtue, who practices it, and who will never step aside from it. I will inform you of my last wishes, and you will execute them punctually if you love me and if you are grateful."

"Oh my father!" I cried, "can you doubt it?"

"No, my dear son, I do not doubt at all. Now listen to me. All these treasures, all the jewels enclosed in this subterranean apartment, also the talismans and the rings, the slaves, and the birds which you have seen are yours. To you Odous," he said to the spirit, "I cannot do more than pronounce all my tenderness for one whom I have found worthy to succeed me. Love him, serve him as you would me, and from the Celestial Sphere to which I shall soon arise, I will watch over you." He clapped his hands and all the slaves appeared. "Here is your master," he said to them. "Be obedient to him, I order you." They all came and prostrated themselves at my feet. "Extend your hand over them as a sign of domination," the old man said to me. I obeyed. They arose, and the old man's having made a sign, they disappeared.

He added, "Take the gold urn which you will find in the cabinet on the right and place it on the table. When I no longer exist, place my body in the middle of this chamber. Take the aromatic woods, which you will find near the coffers filled with gold, and surround me with them. After having poured over the pyre the liquid enclosed in the vase suspended from the roof, you will use the talisman with which I formed the egg in which was enclosed the Black Hen. After having pronounced the mysterious words, you will set the funeral-pile on fire to consume my mortal remains. Take the ashes and enclose them in the urn. Conserve them. Men, cherish my memory; I die content. I would have liked to show you the means of instructing the little Black Pullet, but Heaven which knows our projects has not wished it so.

Odous will teach you; he also knows this secret. I feel my soul ready to fly away. Come, my dear son, dry your tears so that I can press you once again to my heart. Remember, death is only dreaded by the guilty and the unjust man." I approached him and he gave me a last kiss. "Good-bye, my dear son," he said. "Listen to my last wishes." While I was still bending over the sofa, he expired. I could not help myself saying, while sobbing, that the death of the just is sweet and worthy of envy. I fell almost unconscious at the feet of my benefactor.

Odous brought me back to my senses by observing that we had to obey our father. We then punctually performed that which he had ordered, and soon there remained only the ashes of the most just and most virtuous of men.

I said to Odous, "We will leave this day and make all the necessary arrangements for returning to my country.

"I am with you," answered the spirit. "Your wishes are law for me; command and I obey." I had all the slaves brought before me and had them put on French costumes. It sufficed me to have recourse to the talismans. I had all the treasures and the effects which were in the underground vaults transported to the banks of the Nile and provided for the precious urn which I personally kept. Odous found a boat. We went down the river, and very soon we entered the roadstead where a vessel was about to set sail for Marseilles. I boarded with all my people, and soon we were in mid-ocean. The captain of the vessel and the sailors examined us with extreme curiosity. As I spoke all languages at will, they were even more surprised.

Night came and the wind rose. The captain told me that he feared a storm. I told him that his vessel was good and would resist it. That which he foretold arrived; the sea became furious. Fear and despair were on all faces. The pilot could no longer control the ship. Only I, calm and tranquil, seemed unmoved.

Provided with the talisman and ring (Figure No. 9) and pronouncing the mysterious words, I seized the tiller and the vessel which, the instant before, was the plaything of the winds and the surrounding waves, sailed forward lightly over the vast bosom of the sea. The whole crew regarded me as a god, even giving me that name. "I am but man," I told them. "My friends, I do not frighten easily, I know the art of navigation, and you see, it is only necessary to be composed to stand the storm at bay."

The rest of our voyage was very happy. We arrived at Marseilles, and we passed through quarantine before stepping ashore. I paid for my passage and that of my followers with a generosity which astonished the captain. I gave a present to each man of the crew, and I departed crowned with their blessings. I stayed for some time at Marseilles. Having written to the place of my birth, I found that my parents no longer were alive. They had died during my absence leaving me sole heir to their estates which I sold and the proceeds of which were sent to me. I bought a lovely property on the outskirts of Marseilles, the beautiful sky of Provence pleasing me. I improved my house, and I had a delightful stay.

The riches I possessed were such that I could obtain at will all that I desired, even to place myself to my satisfaction. I had a few friends to whom I gave advice, who followed it, and who were all astonished at their prosperity. They were ignorant as to the source. I did not share my secrets with anyone.

Inclination has made me write this little volume. If those who procure it know how to profit from it and are worthy of penetrating the mysteries and the secrets it contains, they will gamble with luck reserved for virtue and wisdom. They must not become discouraged. Constant and stubborn work will surmount everything says an ancient proverb. They should thus work, and if success does not crown their efforts, they must lay the blame on themselves. It is because they are not pure and virtuous. The incredulous, the ignorant, and many others whom it is useless to designate will treat me as a fool, a visionary, an importunist. It matters little to me. The truth is there. I do not seek to repel injuries, still less censure.

Certain family libraries, which have no other merit than to get hold of what belongs to others, will perhaps make haste to publish a surreptitious edition of this work. This is the only thing which I will punish with a talisman which I am keeping to myself and a ring more curious still. I reserve for myself the decoration the perpetrator with two ears six inches longer than those provided of yore for King Midas who had been well judged. It is a warning which I give in passing to certain editors. You notice that for a sorcerer I do not push my vengeance very far.

And you, for whom I have written this work, you who seek to enlighten yourself, to penetrate, to understand the mysteries and the secrets of nature, work with consistency, persevere, purify yourself to obtain success, the object of your wishes and your desires. Consider that the smallest stain with which your heart and your soul will be contaminated will be an invincible obstacle against success. You will see the harbour without being able to enter and will be shipwrecked at the moment when you believe yourself saved. Watch, pray, hope. Adieu my dear and well loved readers. May you be able to play with all the ease which has become my lot. Amen.

The old man did not indicate to me the method of instructing the Black Pullet which he had hatched, but before expiring, he informed me that Odous would impart the important secret to me.

When we were installed in my home in Marseilles, I reminded him of the old man's promise. The Hen was of ordinary size and was eager to satisfy me. It had become so familiar that it hardly ever left me. I took particular care of it during our voyage, and if I have not mentioned this fact, it is because I judged it of little importance. We therefore occupied ourselves with the education of our bird. We placed a piece of gold in the basket where it was in the habit of sleeping and covered its eyes with the hood of which I have already spoken. Two or three days after that preliminary operation, each morning when I took it food to eat, it scratched in its basket, and taking the piece of gold in its beak, it guarded it until I took it.

One can see that the instinct of this bird was as extraordinary as marvelous. Odous said to me, "I have never yet seen as intelligent a one, but also, it is necessary to admit that our good and respected father employed a means to give it birth which was known only to himself and which he had never put into operation in front of me. This proves the tenderness and friendship he had given you. It will be necessary as from tomorrow to hide a piece of gold in the garden. We will carry our Hen to some distance, and we will see if she discovers it." The next morning we did as agreed. I uncovered the head of my bird; it stayed on my knees for some time, looking in different directions. Finally, it jumped lightly to the ground and ran to the foot of a big tree which was opposite us. It started to scratch animatedly. Odous said to me:

"I guarantee that there is some treasure hidden at the foot of that tree. Let the Hen carry on." She scratched all the time and to shorten the operation, I took a spade which the gardner had left nearby, and after having scooped out about two feet, I discovered a case about four feet square and surrounded with iron bands. As we did not have the key, I sent Odous to find the talisman (Figure No. 12). He returned promptly and hardly had I attacked the lock with the ring than it opened, and we discovered several sacks filled with gold and silver, plate, diamonds, jewels, and several other precious objects which were valued at 1,500,000 francs. It seemed that these riches had been concealed in this place during the time of the civil troubles, and as the owners died without revealing their secret, nobody had any knowledge of this deposit. I had bought this property from distant relatives. I could not prevent myself, nor could Odous, from admiring the instinct of our Black Hen, but it was equally necessary for it to find the other piece of hidden gold. We advanced a few steps, and she followed us. Soon she went ahead of us and stopped near the place where the gold was hidden. She soon found it and taking it in her beak, she deposited it at my feet. "Charming bird," I cried! "How precious you are to me. You have put me in the place of a better man, the most tender and respected of fathers to me."

Odous said to me: "See if she will listen to the sacred words which must be pronounced every day to the Black Hen to indicate to her that she must look for things." He then articulated certain words, Nozos, Taraim, Ostus. The Hen appeared to pay attention and to understand because she started to scratch near us and found a ruby mounted in a golden ring. "I am going to pronounce three other words which should indicate to her that she should repose near her master." He then said: Seras, Coristan, Abattuzas. The Hen came and placed herself at my feet. Odous added: "All the hens which you possess know these words but it has taken some time to teach them. One must hold them with a ribbon: when pronouncing the first words, one must make them walk; when pronouncing the second, one stops them. As these birds are endowed with a particular instinct, they then do that which one desires."

Having the casket brought in by my slaves, I added the Pullet's findings to those which I already possessed.

I had an elegant pavilion constructed of Cremona marble, and I placed the urn containing the ashes of the old man on a black marble pedestal with a silver plaque which expressed my recognition and regrets. I had cypresses and weeping willows planted, and every day at the rising of the sun, I went, followed by Odous, to visit this pavilion and to pass an hour in support of our good father, remembering the lessons and examples of virtue which he had given me. I will cite several events with great solemnity: that on which he saved my life by taking me into the Pyramid and the anniversary of his death. This day was consecrated to grief and meditation in my house. And once every year all my slaves entered the drove which I had had surrounded with a metal grill so that nobody could enter. Also, the thickness of the bushes and the winding paths which had to be wandered through before arriving at the pavilion prevented the most piercing eye from seeing it. My days passed between work, study, meditation, and walking exercise. I received a few visitors in my home, but nobody had an inkling of that which passed in my private life. To live happily, live concealed, as a Sage said. And this proverb is the rule and foundation of my conduct.

FINIS

THE GRIMOIRE OF HONORIUS

THE GRIMOIRE OF HONORIUS

The person who desires to invoke the perverse "Spirits of Darkness must observe a three days' fast; he must also confess and approach the Holy Altar. After these three days, upon the morrow, and at the hour of sunrise, he shall recite the Seven Gradual Psalms, with the accoinpanying Litanies and Prayers,1 the whole on his knees; further, he must drink no wine and eat no meat on that day. Next, he shall rise at midnight on the first Monday of the month, and a priest shall say a Mass of the Holy Ghost. After the consecration, taking the Host in his left hand, he shall recite the following prayer on his knees:

PRAYER

My Sovereign Saviour Jesus Christ, Son of the living God! Thou who for the salvation of all mankind didst suffer the death of the Cross; Thou who, before being abandoned to Thine enemies, by an impulse of ineffable love didst institute the Sacrament of thy Body; Thou who hast vouchsafed to us miserable creatures the privilege of making daily commemoration thereof; do Thou deign unto thine unworthy servant, thus holding thy Living Body in his hands, all strength and ability for the profitable application of that power with which he has been entrusted against the horde of rebellious spirits. Thou art their true God, and if they tremble at the utterance of Thy Name, upon that Holy Name will I call, crying Jesus Christ! Jesus, be Thou my help, now and for ever! Amen.

After sunrise a black cock must be killed, the first feather of its left wing being plucked and preserved for use at the required time. The eyes must be torn out, and so also the tongue and heart; these must be dried in the sun and afterwards reduced to powder. The remains must be interred at sunset in a secret place, a cross of a palm in height being set upon the mound, while at each of the four corners the signs which here follow must be drawn with the thumb :

℞ ⸱ ⁓ 9 ☨ 2 ⸱ 7 On this day also the operator should drink no wine and abstain from eating meat.

On Tuesday, at break of day, let him say a Mass of the Angels,[1] placing the feather taken from the bird upon the altar, together with a new penknife. The signs hereinafter represented must be inscribed on a sheet of clean paper with the consecrated wine which is the Blood of Jesus Christ:

They should be written upon the altar, and at the end of the Mass the paper should be folded in a new veil of violet silk, to be concealed on the morrow, together with the oblation of the Mass and a part of the consecrated Host.

On the evening of Thursday the operator must rise at midnight, and, having sprinkled holy water about the chamber, he must light a taper of yellow wax, which shall have been prepared on the Wednesday and pierced in the form of a cross. When it is lighted he shall recite Psalm lxxvii.2—Attendite, popule meus, legem meam, &c.—without the Gloria Patri. He shall then begin the "Office of the Dead" with 1/enite exultemus Domino, &c. He shall recite Matins and Lauds, but in place of the versicle of the ninth Lesson 1 he shall say:

Deliver us, O Lord, from the fear of hell. Let not the demons destroy my soul when I shall raise them from the deep pit, when I shall command them to do my will. May the day be bright, may

---

[1] The Mass for the Apparition of St. Michael, May 8, with a special Epistle, Gospel, Commemoration, &c,

the sun and moon shine forth, when I shall call upon them. Terrible of aspect are they, deformed and horrible to sight; but do Thou restore unto them their angelic shapes when I shall impose my will upon them. o Lord deliver me from those of the dread visage, and grant that they shall be obedient when I shall raise them up from hell, when I shall impose my will upon them.

After the "Office of the Dead" the operator shall extinguish the taper, and at sunrise shall cut the throat of a male lamb of nine days, taking care that the blood does not gush forth upon the earth. He shall skin the lamb, and shall cast its tongue and heart into the fire. The fire must be freshly kindled, and the ashes shall be preserved for use at the proper time. The skin of th~ lamb shall be spread in the middle of a field, and for the space of nine days shall be sprinkled four times every day with holy water. On the tenth day, before the rising of the sun, the lambskin shall be covered with the ashes of the heart and tongue, and with the ashes also of the cock. On Thursday, after sunset, the flesh of the lamb shall be interred in a secret place where no bird can come, and the priest with his right thumb shall inscribe on the grave the characters here indicated

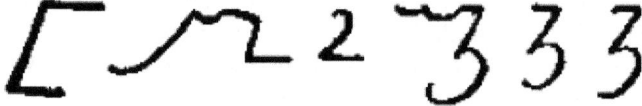

Moreover, for the space of three days he shall sprinkle the four corners with holy water, saying: Sprinkle me, o Lord, with hyssop, and I shall be cleansed! Wash me, and I shall be made whiter than snow!

After the aspersion let him recite the following prayer, kneeling with his face towards the east

PRAYER

Christ Jesus, Redeemer of men, who, being the Lamb without spot, wast immolated for the salvation of the human race, who alone wast found worthy to open the Book of Life, impart such virtue to this lambskin that it may receive the signs which we shall trace thereon, written with Thy blood, so that the figures, signs, and words may become efficacious; and grant that this skin may preserve us against the wiles of the demons; that they may be terrified at the sight of these figures, and may only approach them trembling. Through Thee, Jesus Christ, who livest and reignest through all ages. So be it.

The Litanies of the Holy Name of Jesus must then be repeated, but instead of the Agnus Del, substitute:

Immolated Lamb, be Thou a pillar of strength against the demons Slain Lamb, give power over the Powers of Darkness! Immolated Lamb, grant favour and strength unto the binding of the Rebellious Spirits. So be it.

The lambskin shall be stretched for eighteen days, and on the nineteenth day the fleece shall be removed, reduced into powder, and interred in the same place. The word vellus shall be written above it with the finger, together with the following character and the words: May this which hath been reduced into ashes preserve against the demons through the name of Jesus.

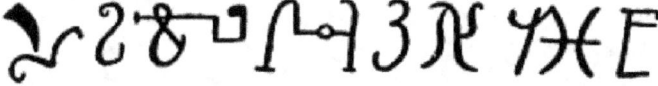

Add also these signs

Lastly, on the eastern side, the said skin must be set to dry in the sun for three days, the ensuing characters being cut with a new knife:

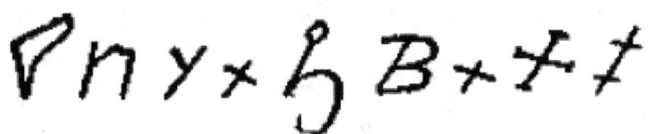

— This being accomplished, recite Psalm lxxi., Deus, judicium tuum regi da, &c., and cut the following characters

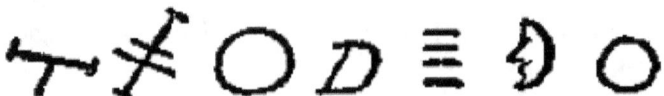

The figure being thus far completed, recite the verses *Afferte Domino, patria' gentium,* occurring in Psalm xcv.: *Cantate Domino Canticum novum,* of which the seventh versicle is: *Off erte Domino, Full Del,* &c., and cut subsequently these characters:

— Next recite Psalm lxxvii.: *Attendite, popule meus, legem meam,* and compose the following figure:

— Which being accomplished, recite Psalm ii.: *Quart' fre,nuerunt gentes et populi ineditati sunt inaniaP* Then make another figure as follows

And recite Psalm cxv.: (_redidi pro pter quod locutus sum. Finally, on the last day of the month a Mass for the Dead shall be offered; the prose shall be omitted, and also the Gospel of St. John, but at the end of the Mass the priest shall recite the Psalm *Confitemini Domino quoniam bonus,* &c.

In Honour of the Most Holy and August Trinity, the Father, the Son, and the Holy Ghost. Amen.

THE SEVENTY-TWO SACRED NAMES OF GOD

—TRINITAS, SOTHER, MESSIAS, EMMANUEL, SABAHOT, ADONAY, ATHANATOS, JESU, PENTAGNA, ARGAGON, ISCHIROS, ELEYSON, OTHEOS, TETRAGRAMMATON, ELY, SADAY, AQUILA, MAGNUS HOMO, *Vzsro,* FLOS, ORIGO, SALVATOR, ALPHIA AND OMEGA, PRIMIJS, NovissIMus, PRINI At this point the process of the Grimoire becomes almost unintelligible. The relation of the seventy-two names apparently succeeds the Psalm, and is followed by the Second Gospel, which is not omitted after all. There is then an extension of the *Deo Gratias;* this concluded the Mass, which seems immediately followed by the evocation. But the use of the Pentacles of Solomon and St. John does not appear, in the one case, till the close of the Conjurations, and not at all in the other.

CIPIUM ET FINIS, PRIMOGENITUS, SAPIENTIA, VIRTUS, PARACLITUS, VERITAS, VIA, MEDIATOR, MEDICUS, SALUS, AGNUS, OVIS, VITULUS, SPES, ARIES, LEO, LUX, IMAGO, PANIS, JANUA, PETRA, SPONSA, PASTOR, PROPHETA, SACERDOS, SANCTUS, IMMORTALITAS, JESUS, CHRISTUS, PATER, FILIUS HoMINIS, SANCTUS, PATER OMNIPOTENS, DEUS, AGIOS, RESSURRECTIO, MISCRIROS, CHARITAS, AETERNAS, CREATOR, REDEM PTOR, UNITAS, SUM MUM BONUM, INFINITAS. AMEN.

Hereinafter follow the three small pentacles of Solomon, and that of the Gospel of St. John.

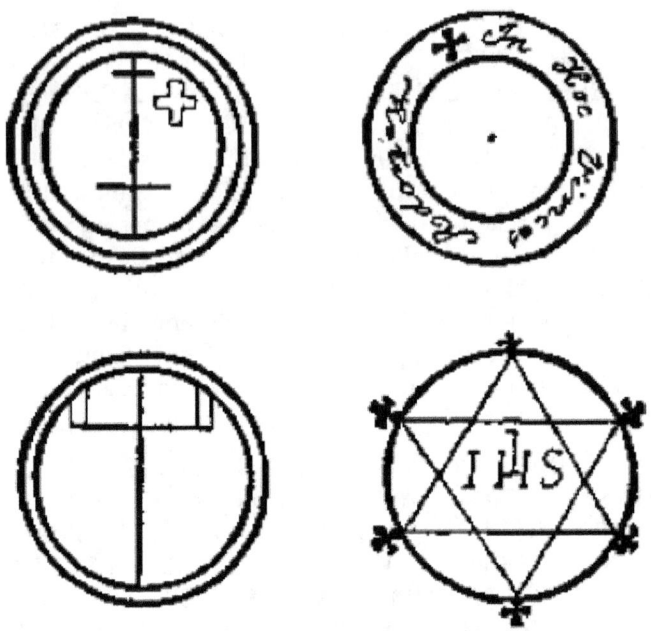

THE BEGINNING OF THE HOLY GOSPEL ACCORDING TO JOHN

Glory be to Thee, o Lord.

In the beginning was the Word, &c., in extenso, so far as the end of the fourteenth versicle.

Thanks be to God. Hosanna to the Son of David!

Blessed is He who cometh in the Name of the Lord.

Hosanna in the Highest. We invoke Thee. We adore Thee. We praise Thee. We glorify Thee, o blessed and glorious Trinity! May the Name of the Lord be blessed, now and henceforth for ever! Amen. In the Name of the Father, of the Son, and of the Holy Ghost, Jesus of Nazareth, King of the Jews. May Christ conquer, reign, command, and defend me from all evil. Amen.

UNIVERSAL CONJURATION

I, N., do conjure thee, o Spirit N., by the living God, by the true God, by the holy and all-ruling God, who created from nothingness the heaven, the earth, the sea, and all things that are therein, in virtue of the Most Holy Sacrament of the Eucharist, in the name of Jesus Christ, and by the power of this same Almighty Son of God, who for us and for our redemption was crucified, suffered death, and was buried; who rose again on the third day, and is now seated on the right hand of the Creator of the whole world, from whence he will come to judge the living and the dead; as also by the precious love of the Holy Spirit, perfect Trinity. I conjure thee within the circle, accursed one, by thy judgment, who didst dare to tempt God: I exorcise thee, Serpent, and I command thee to appear forthwith under a beautiful and well-favoured human form of soul and body, and to fulfil my behests without any deceit whatsoever, as also without mental reservation of any kind, by the great times of the God of gods and Lord of lords, ADONAY, TETRAGRAM MATON, JEHOVA, TETRAGRAM MATON, ADONAY, JEHOVA, OTHEOS, ATHANATOS, ISCHYRoS, AGLA, PENTACRAM MATON, SADAY, SADAY, SADAY, JEHOVA, OTHEOS, ATHANATOS a Liciat TETRAGRAMMATON, ADONAY, ISCHYROS, ATHANATOS, SADY, SADY, SADY, CADOS, CADOS, CADOS, ELOY. AGLA, AGLA, AGLA, ADONAY, ADONAY.

I conjure thee, Evil and Accursed Serpent, N.. to appear at my will and pleasure, in this place, before this circle, without tarrying, without companions, without grievance, without noise, deformity, or murmuring. I exorcise thee by the ineffable names of God, to wit, Gog and Magog, which I am unworthy to pronounce; Come hither, Conic hither, Come hither.

Accomplish my will and desire, without wile or falsehood. Otherwise St. Michael, the invisible Archangel, shall presently blast thee in the utmost depths of hell. Come, then, N., to do my will.

THE GRAND PENTACLE OF SALOMON

A.P.

Why tarriest thou, and why delayest? What doest thou? Make ready, obey your master, in the name of the Lord, BATHAT or RACHAT flowing over ABRACM ENS, ALCHOR or ABERER.

L. Q. L. F. A. P.

Behold the Pentacle of Solomon which I have brought into thy presence! I command thee, by order of the great God, ADONAY, TETRAGRAMMATON, and JEsUs!

Hasten, fulfil my behests, without wile or falsehood, but in all truth, in the name of the Saviour and Redeemer, Jesus Christ.

DISCHARGE.

Go in peace unto your places. May there be peace between us and you, and be ye ready to come when ye are called. In the Name of the Father, and of the Son, and of the Holy Ghost. Amen.

ACT OF THANKSGIVING

Praise, honour, glory, and blessing be unto Him who sitteth upon the throne, who liveth for ever and ever. Amen.

CONJURATION OF THE BOOK

I conjure thee, o Book, to be useful and profitable unto all who shall have recourse to thee for the success of their affairs. I conjure thee anew, by the virtue of the Blood of Jesus Christ, contained daily in the chalice, to be serviceable unto all those who shall read thee. I exorcise thee, in the name of the Most Holy Trinity, in the name of the Most Holy Trinity, in the name of the Most Holy Trinity!

What follows must be said before the sealing of the Book.

I conjure and command you, o Spirits, all and so many as ye are, to accept this Book with good grace, so that whensoever we may read it, the same being approved and recognised as in proper form and valid, you shall be constrained to appear in comely human form when you are called, accordingly as the reader shall judge. In no circumstances shall you make any attempt upon the body, soul, or spirit of the reader, nor inflict any harm on those who may accompany him, either by mutterings, tempests, noise, scandals, nor yet by lesion or by hindrance in the execution of the commands of this Book. I conjure you to appear immediately when the conjuration is made, to execute without dallying all that is written and enumerated in its proper place in the said book. You shall obey, serve, instruct, impart, and perform all in your power for the benefit of those who command you, and the whole without illusion. If perchance some of the invoked spirits be unable to come or appear when required, they shall be bound over to send others vested with their power, who also shall swear solemnly to execute all that the reader may demand, and ye are all hereby enjoined by the Most Holy Names of the Omnipotent Living God, ELOYM, JAH, EL, ELOY, TETRAGRAMMATON, to fulfil everything as it is set forth above. If ye obey me not, I will force you to abide in torments for a thousand years, as also if any one of you receive not this Book with entire resignation to the will of the reader.

CONJURATION OF THE DEMONS

In the Name of the Father, and of the Son, and of the Holy Ghost. Take heed! Come, all Spirits! By the virtue and power of your King, and by the seven crowns and chains of your Kings, all Spirits of the Hells are forced to appear in my presence before this pentacle or circle of Solomon, whensoever I shall call them. Come, then, all at my orders, to fulfil that which is in your power, as commanded. Come, therefore, from the East, South, West, and North! I conjure and command you, by the virtue and power of Him who is three, eternal, equal, who is God invisible, consubstantial, in a word, who has created the heavens, the sea, and all which is under heaven.

After these Conjurations you shall command them to affix the Seal.

CONCERNING THE FIGURE OF THE CIRCLE

Circles should be described with charcoal or holy water, sprinkled with the wood of the blessed Cross.

THE MAGIC CIRCLE OF HONORIUS

When they have been duly made, and the words have been written about the circle, the holy water which has served to bless the same may also be used to prevent the spirits from inflicting any hurt. Standing in the middle of the circle, you shall command them in a lively manner, as one who is their master.

What must be said in Composing the Circle. o Lord, we fly to Thy virtue! o Lord, confirm this work! What is operated in us becomes like dust driven before the wind, and the Angel of the Lord pausing (sic), let the darkness disappear, and the Angel of the Lord ever pursuing, ALPHA, OMEGA, ELY, ELOTHE, FLOHIM, ZABAHOT, FLION, SADY. Behold the Lion who is the conqueror of the Tribe of Judah, the Root of David! I will open the Book, and the seven seals thereof.

I have beheld Satan as a bolt falling from heaven. It is Thou who hast given us power to crush dragons, scorpions, and all Thine enemies beneath Thy feet. Nothing shall harm us, not even ELOY, ELOHIM, ELOHE, ZABAHOT, ELIoN, ESARCHIE, ADONAY, JAH, TETRAGRAMMATON, SADY. The earth is the Lord's and all those who dwell therein, because He established it upon the seas and prepared it in the midst of the waves. Who shall ascend unto the mountain of the Lord? Who shall be received in his Holy Place? The innocent of hands and clean of heart. Who bath not received his soul in vain, and hath not sworn false witness against his neighbour. The same shall be blessed of God, and shall obtain mercy of God to his salvation. He is of the generation of those who seek Him. Open your gates, ye princes, open the eternal gates, and the King of Glory shall enter! Who is this King of Glory? The Lord Almighty, the Lord, mighty in battle. Open your gates, ye princes! Lift up the eternal gates. Who is this King of Glory? The Lord Almighty. This Lord is the King of Glory. Glory be to the Father, &c.

To dismiss them, the Pentacle of Solomon must be exhibited, at the same time saying a-s follows:— Behold your sentence! Behold that which forbids rebellion to our wills, and doth ordain you to return unto your abodes. May peace be between us and you, and be my will.

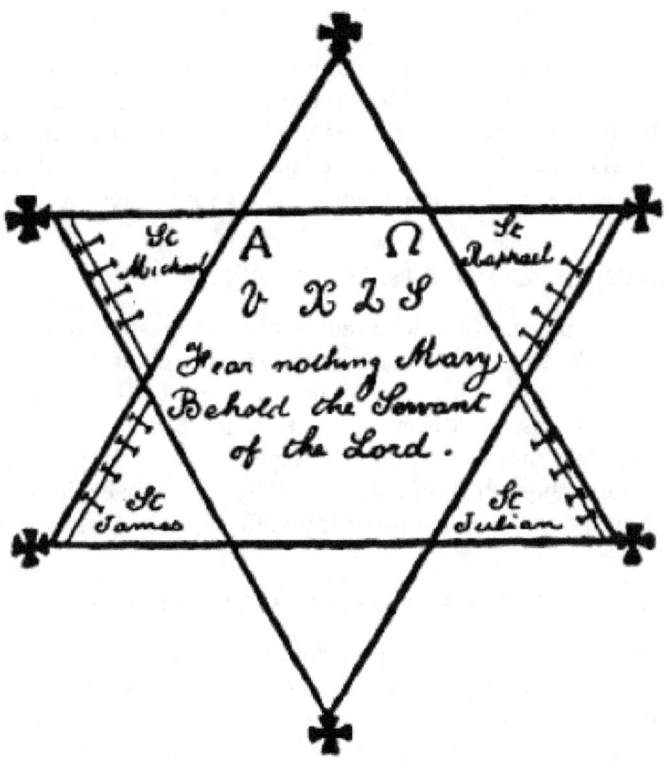

CONJURATION OF THE KING OF THE EAST

I conjure and invoke thee, o powerful King of the East Magoa, by my holy labour, by all the names of Divinity, by the name of the All-Powerful: I command thee to obey, and to come to me, or that failing, forthwith and immediately to send unto me Massayel, Ariel, Satiel, Arduel, Acorib, to respond concerning all that I would know and to fulfil all that I shall command. Else thou shalt come verily in thine own person to satisfy my will; which refusing, I shall compel thee by all the virtue and power of God.

The Grand Pentacle or Circle of Solomon will answer for the above and following Conjurations, which can be said on all days and at all hours. If it be desired to speak only with one spirit, one only need be named, at the choice of the reader.

CONJURATION OF THE KING OF THE SOUTH

o Egym, great King of the South, I conjure and invoke thee by the most high and holy Names of God, do thou here manifest, clothed with all thy power; come before this circle, or at least send me forthwith Fadal, Nastrache, to make answer unto me, and to execute all my wishes. If thou failest, I shall force thee by God Himself.

CONJURATION OF THE KING OF THE WEST

o Baymon, most potent King, who reignest in the Western quarter, I call and I invoke thee in the name of the Deity! I command thee by virtue of the Most High, to send me immediately before this circle the Spirit Passiel Rosus, with all other Spirits who are subject unto thee, that the same may answer in everything, even as I shall require them. If thou failest, I will torment thee with the sword of fire divine; I will multiply thy sufferings, and will burn thee.

CONJURATION OF THE KING OF THE NORTH

O thou, Amaymon, King and Emperor of the Northern parts, I call, invoke, exorcise, and conjure thee, by the virtue and power of the Creator, and by the virtue of virtues, to send me presently, and without delay, Madael, Laaval, Bamlahe, Belem, and Ramath, with all other Spirits of thine obedience, in comely and human form! In whatsoever place thou now art, come hither and render that honour which thou owest to the true living God, who is thy Creator. In the name of the Father, of the Son, and of the Holy Ghost, come therefore, and be obedient, in front of this circle, without peril to my body or soul. Appear in comely human form, with no terror encompassing thee. I conjure thee, make haste, come straightway, and at once. By all the Divine names—SECHIEL, BARACHIEL—if thou dost not obey promptly, BALANDIER, suspensus, iracundus, Origratiumgu, Partus, Olemdemis, and Bautratis, N. I exorcise thee, do invoke, and do impose most high commandment upon thee, by the omnipotence of the living God, and of the true God; by the virtue of the holy God, and by the power of Him who spake and all things were made, even by His holy commandment the heaven and earth were made, with all that is in them! I adjure thee by the Father, by the Son, and by the Holy Ghost, even by the Holy Trinity, by that God whom thou canst not resist, under whose empire I will compel thee; I conjure thee by God the Father, by God the Son, by God the Holy Ghost, by the Mother of Jesus Christ, Holy Mother and perpetual Virgin, by her sacred heart, by her blessed milk, which the Son of the Father sucked, by her most holy body and soul, by all the parts and members of this Virgin, by all the sufferings, afflictions, labours, agonies which she endured during the whole course of her life, by all the sighs she uttered, by the holy tears which she shed whilst her dear Son wept before the time of His dolorous passion and on the tree of the Cross, by all the sacred holy things which are offered and done, and also by all others, as in heaven so on earth, in honour of our Saviour Jesus Christ, and of the Blessed Mary, His Mother, by whatsoever is celestial, by the Church Militant, in honour of the Virgin and of all the Saints. In like manner, I conjure thee by the Holy Trinity, by all other mysteries, by the sign of the Cross, by the most precious blood and water which flowed from the side of Jesus Christ, by the sweat which issued from His whole body, when He said in the Garden of Olives: My Father, if it be possible, let this chalice pass from me— I conjure thee by His death and passion, by His burial and glorious resurrection, by His ascension, by the coming of the Holy Ghost. I adjure thee, furthermore, by the crown of thorns which was set upon His head, by the blood which flowed from His feet and hands, by the nails with which He was nailed to the tree of the Cross, by the holy tears which He shed, by all which He suffered willingly through great love of us: by the lungs, the heart, the hair, the inward parts, and by all the members, of our Saviour Jesus Christ. I conjure thee by the judgment of the living and the dead, by the Gospel words of our Saviour Jesus Christ, by His preachings, by His sayings, by all His miracles, by the child in swaddling-clothes, by the crying child, borne by the mother in her most pure and virginal womb; by the glorious intercession of the Virgin Mother of our Saviour Jesus Christ; by all which is of God and of His Most Holy Mother, as in heaven so on earth. I conjure thee by the holy Angels and Archangels, and by all the blessed orders of Spirits, by the holy patriarchs and prophets, by all the holy martyrs and confessors, by all the holy virgins and innocent widows, and by all the saints of God, both men and women. I conjure thee by the head of St. John the Baptist, by the milk of St. Catherine, and by all the Saints.

CONJURATION FOR EACH DAY OF THE WEEK

FOR MONDAY, TO LUCIFER.

This experience is commonly performed between eleven and twelve o'clock, or between three and four. Requisites: coal, and consecrated chalk to compose the circle, about which these words must be written: I forbid thee, Lucifer, in the name of the Most Holy Trinity, to enter within this circle. A mouse must be provided to give him; the master must have a stole and holy water, an air also and a surplice. He must recite the Conjuration in a lively manner, commanding sharply and shortly, as a lord should address his servant, with all kinds of menaces: SATAN, RANTAM, PALLANTRE, LUTAIS, CoRICACOEM, SCIRCIGREUR, I require thee to give me very humbly, &c.

CONJURATION

I conjure thee, Lucifer, by the living God, by the true God, by the holy God, who spake and all was made, who commanded and all things were created and made! I conjure thee by the ineffable name of God, ON, ALPHA and OMEGA, ELOY, ELOYM, YA, SADAY, LUX, MUGIENS, REX, SALUS, ADONAY, EMMANUEL, MEssIAs; and I adjure, conjure, and exorcise thee by the names which are declared under the letters V, C, X, as also by the names JEHOVAH, SOL, AGLA, RIFFAsoRIs, ORIsToN, ORPHITNE, PHATON, IPRETU, OCIA, SP1~RATON, IMAGON, AMUL, PENATON, SOTER, TETRAGRAMMATON, ELOY, PREMOTON, SITMON, PERIGARON, IRATATON, PLEGATON, ON, PEROHIRAM, TIRos, RUBIPHATON, SIMULATON, PERPI, KLARIMUM, TREMENDUM, MERAY, and by the most high ineffable names of God, GALl, ENGA, EL, HABDANUM, INGODUM, OBU ENGLABIS, do thou make haste to come, or send me N., having a comely and human form in no wise repulsive, that he may answer in real truth whatsoever I shall ask him, being also powerless to hurt me, or any person whomsoever, either in body or soul.

FOR TUESDAY, TO FRIMOST.

This experience is performed at night from nine to ten o'clock, and the first stone found is given to him. He is to be received with dignity and honour. Proceed as on Monday; compose the circle, and write about it:

Obey me, Frimost! Obey me, Frimost! Obey me, Frimost!

CONJURATION

I conjue and command thee, Frimost, by all the names wherewith thou canst be constrained and bound! I exorcise thee, Nambroth, by thy name, by the virtue of all spirits, by all characters, by the Jewish, Greek, and Chaldean conjurations, by the confusion and malediction, and I will redouble thy pains and torments from day to day for ever, if thou come not now to accomplish my will and submit to all that I shall command, being powerless to harm me, or those who accompany me, either in body or soul.

FOR WEDNESDAY, TO ASTAROTH.

This experience is performed at night, from ten to eleven o'clock; it is designed to obtain the good graces of the King and others. Write in the circle as follows:

Come, Astaroth! Come, Astaroth! Come, Astaroth!

CONJURATION

I conjure thee, Astaroth, wicked spirit, by the words Christ of Nazareth, unto whom all demons are submitted, who was conceived of the Virgin Mary; by the mystery of the Angel Gabriel, I conjure thee; and again in the name of the Father, and of the Son, and of the Holy Ghost; in the name of the glorious Virgin Mary, and of the Most Holy Trinity, in whose honour do all the Archangels, Thrones, Dominations, Powers, Patriarchs, Prophets, Apostles, and Evangelists sing without end; Hosannah, Hosannah, Hosannah, Lord God of Hosts, who art, who wast, who art to come, as a river of burning fire! Neglect not my commands, refuse not to come. I command thee by Him who shall appear with flames to judge the living and the dead, unto whom is all honour, praise, and glory.

Come, therefore, promptly, obey my will, appear and give praise to the true God, unto the living God, yea, unto all His works; fail not to obey me, and give honour to the Holy Ghost, in whose name I command thee.

This experience is made at night, from three to four o'clock, at which hour he is called, and appears in the form of a King. A little bread must be given him when he is required to depart; he renders man happy and also discovers treasures. Write about the circle as follows: Holy God! Holy God! Holy God!

CONJURATION

I conjure thee, Silcharde, by the image and likeness of Jesus Christ our Saviour, whose death and passion redeemed the entire human race, who also wills that, by His providence, thou appear forthwith in this place. I command thee by all the Kingdoms of God. Act—I adjure and constrain thee by his Holy Name, by Him who walked upon the asp, who crushed the lion and the dragon. Do thou obey me, and fulfil my commands, being powerless to do harm unto me, or any person whomsoever, either in body or soul.

FOR FRIDAY, TO BECHARD.

This experience is peformed an night from eleven to twelve o'clock, and a nut must be given to him. Write within the circle: Come, Bechard! Come, Bechard! Come, Bechard!

CONJURATION

I conjure thee, Bechard, and constrain thee, in like manner, by the Most Holy Names of God, ELOY, ADONAY, ELOY, AGLA, SAMALABACTAY, which are written in Hebrew, Greek and Latin; by all the sacraments, by all the names written in this book; and by him who drove thee from the height of Heaven. I conjure and command thee by the virtue of the Most Holy Eucharist, which hath redeemed men from their sins; I conjure thee to come without any delay, to do and perform all my biddings, without any prejudice to my body or soul, without harming my book, or doing injury to those that accompany me.

FOR SATURDAY, TO GULAND.

This experience is performed at night from eleven to twelve o'clock, and so soon as he appears burnt bread must be given him. Ask him anything you will, and he will obey you on the spot. Write in his circle: Enter not, Guland! Enter not, Guland! Enter not, Guland!

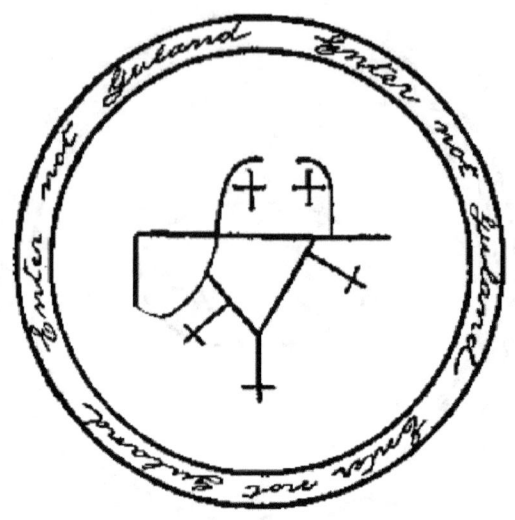

CONJURATION

I conjure thee, o Guland, in the name of Satan, in the name of Beelzebuth, in the name of Astaroth, and in the name of all other Spirits, to make haste and appear before me. Come, then in the name of Satan and in the names of all other demons. Come to me, I command thee, in the name of the Most Holy Trinity. Come without inflicting any harm upon me, without injury to my body or soul, without maltreating my books, or anything which I use. I command thee to appear without delay, or, that failing, to send me forthwith another Spirit having the same power as thou hast, who shall accomplish my commands and be submitted to my will, wanting which, he whom thou shalt send me, if indeed thou comest not thyself, shall in no wise depart, nor until he bath in all things fulfilled my desire.

FOR SUNDAY, TO SURGAT.

This experience is performed at night from eleven to one o'clock. He will demand a hair of your head, but give him one of a fox, and see that he takes it. His office is to discover and transport all treasures, and perform anything that you may will. Write in his circle: TnTRAGRAM MATON, TETRAGRAM MATON,

TETRAGRAM MATON. ISMAEL, ADONAY, IHUA. And in a second circle: Come, Surgat! Come, Surgat t Come, Surgat!

CONJURATION

I conjure thee, o Surgat, by all the names which are written in this book, to present thyself here before me, promptly and without delay, being ready to obey me in all things, or, failing this, to despatch me a Spirit with a stone which shall make me invisible to every one whensoever I carry it! And I conjure thee to be submitted in thine own person, or in the person of him or of those whom thou shalt send me, to do and accomplish my will, and all that I shall command, without harm to me or to any one, so soon as I make known my intent.

Very Powerful Conjuration for all days and hours of the Day or Night, being for Treasures hidden by men or Spirits, that the same may be possessed and transported.

I command you, o all ye demons dwelling in these parts, or in what part of the world soever ye may be, by whatsoever power may have been given you by God and our holy Angels over this place, and by the powerful Principality of the infernal abysses, as also by all your brethren, both general and special demons, whether dwelling in the East, West, South, or North, or in any side of the earth, and, in like manner, by the power of God the Father, by the wisdom of God the Son, by the virtue of the Holy Ghost, and by the authority I derive from our Saviour Jesus Christ, the only Son of the Almighty and the Creator, who made us and all creatures from nothing, who also ordains that you do hereby abdicate all power to guard, habit, and abide in this place; by whom further I constrain and command you, *nolens volens*, without guile or deception, to declare me your names, and to leave me in peaceable possession and rule over this place, of whatsoever legion you be and of whatsoever part of the world; by order of the Most Holy Trinity, and by the merits of the Most Holy and Blessed Virgin, as also of all the saints, I unbind you all, spirits who abide in this place, and I drive you to the deepest infernal abysses. Thus: Go, all Spirits accursed, who are condemned to the flame eternal which is prepared for you and your companions, if ye be rebellious and disobedient. I conjure you by the same authority, I exhort and call you, I constrain and command you, by all the powers of your superior demons, to come, obey, and reply positively to what I direct you in the name of Jesus Christ. Whence, if you or they do not obey promptly and without tarrying, I will shortly increase your torments for a thousand years in hell. I constrain you therefore to appear here in comely human shape, by the Most High Names of God, HAIN, LoN, HILAY, SABAOTH, HELIM, RADISH~~, LEDIEHA, ADONAY, JEHOVA, YAH, TETRAGRAMMATON, SADA!, MESSIAS, AGIOS, ISCHYROS, EMMANUEL, AGLA, Jesus who is ALPHA and OMEGA, the beginning and the end, that you be justly established in the fire, having no power to reside, habit, or abide in this place henceforth; and I require your doom by the virtue of the said names, to wit, that St. Michael drive you to the uttermost of the infernal abyss, in the name of the Father, and of the Son, and of the Holy Ghost. So I conjure thee, Acham, or whomsoever thou mayst be, by the Most Holy Names of God, by MALHAME, JAE, MAY, MABRON, JACOB, DASMEDIAS, ELoY, ATERESTIN, JANASTARDY, FINI5, AGIos, JSCHYROS, OTHEOS, ATHANATOS, AGLA, JEHOVA, HOMoSION, AGA, MESSIAS, SOTHER, CHRISTUS VINCIT, CHRISTUS IMPERAT, INCREATUS SPIRITUS SANCTUS.

I conjure thee, Cassiel, or whomsoever thou mayst be, by all the said names, with power and with exorcism! I warn thee by the other sacred names of the most great Creator, which are or shall hereafter be communicated to thee; hearken forthwith and immediately to my words, and observe them inviolably, as sentences of the last dreadful day of judgment, which thou must obey inviolately, nor think to repulse me because I am a sinner, for therein shalt thou repulse the commands of the Most High God. Knowest thou not that thou art bereft of thy powers before thy Creator and ours? Think therefore what thou refusest, and pledge therefore thine obedience, swearing by the said last dreadful day of judgment, and by Him who bath created all things by His word, whom all creatures obey. P. *per sedem Balda'rey et per gratiam et diligentiam tuam habuisti ab eo ha~ic n&atimanamilam,* as I command thee.

www.ingramcontent.com/pod-product-compliance
Lightning Source LLC
Chambersburg PA
CBHW050339230426
43663CB00010B/1924